REVELATION FOR LENT

RESOURCES FOR LENT-EASTER PREACHING AND WORSHIP BASED ON REVELATION 2:1–3:22

DONALD H. NEIDIGK

CONCORDIA PUBLISHING HOUSE · SAINT LOUIS

Copyright © 2004 Concordia Publishing House
3558 S. Jefferson Avenue
St. Louis, Missouri 63118-3968

All Scripture quotations are taken from the HOLY BIBLE, NEW INTERNATIONAL VERSION®. NIV®.
Copyright © 1973, 1978, 1984 by International Bible Society. Used by permission of Zondervan
Publishing House.

The SymbolGREEK II font used to print this work is available from Linguist's Software, Inc.,
PO Box 580, Edmonds, WA 98020-0580, USA; telephone (425) 775-1130; www.linguistsoftware.com.

Manufactured in the United States of America

Library of Congress Cataloging-in-Publication Data
  Neidigk, Donald, 1949–
      Revelation for Lent : resources for Lent-Easter preaching and worship based
  on Revelation 2:1–3:22 / Donald H. Neidigk.
          p. cm.
       ISBN 0-7586-0751-2
    1. Lenten sermons. I. Title.
       BV4277.N375 2004
       251'.62—dc22   2004004864

2   3   4   5   6   7   8   9   10   11   14   13   12   11   10   09   08   07   06   05

CONTENTS

INTRODUCTION

Has it ever crossed your mind that your congregation might have its own angel? That's not such a far-fetched idea, especially because the apostle John was instructed by the Lord Jesus Christ to write letters to the angels of seven churches in Asia (Revelation 1:10ff.). It is not absolutely certain that the angels to whom John refers are heavenly beings. Some scholars believe them to be pastors. But others consider them literally to be angels sent by God from heaven to do His will for the preservation and growth of His people. Just imagine your own congregation with its very own angel! Wouldn't it be comforting to know that God is taking care of you and your congregation like that?

To avoid misunderstanding the biblical witness about angels, consider that in the nineteenth and twentieth centuries, the belief that God created real angels had largely ceased. Scholars considered biblical language about angels to be metaphorical or psychological. Of course, the Bible gives witness to angels, and we take God at His word. God really did make angels, but not necessarily like those portrayed in the media. At some point during the six-day work of creation, God created the angels. They rejoiced and sang the praises of God's work, as suggested by Job 38:7. However, angels did not participate with God in the act of creation, which is of God alone (John 1:1–3). The word *angel* means "messenger" and primarily describes the office that these heavenly beings fulfill. Malachi 2:7 calls those whom God has chosen to proclaim His word "angels." Clearly, the emphasis is on the message—God's Word. Even as Christ, known in the Old Testament as the Angel of the Lord, provides the focus for all that is revealed from the Father, so all the other angels witness to and serve Him. They cannot take glory from the Lord, under whose word, both written and in Christ, they stand. Angels are powerful yet modest. They are immaterial yet frightening to those to whom they reveal themselves. The holy angels serve in God's army and do His bidding without sin.

The devil and the wicked "angels," or demons, seek their own glory. Hell was originally meant to be the eternal dwelling of these wicked angels. Like sinful people under God's word of Law, these wicked angels turned away from God and merited His eternal wrath. God's great favor shown to us as He saves us in Christ Jesus was not extended to the wicked angels. When a third of all angels fell into sin, they fell utterly and forever (see Revelation 12:4).

All creatures, whether heavenly or earthly, stand under God. Merely being incorporeal or "spiritual" does not make angels better than human beings. That is a myth of pagan origin that says flesh is evil while spirit is good. Yet Christ took up the tabernacle of human flesh and dwelt among us (John 1:14).

Angels may assist in caring for God's people, yet they never replace God. They do not act as a means to provide the pastor or anyone else with God's message of Law and Gospel (Galatians 1:8–9). We receive the Gospel solely from the Holy Spirit through the means of Word and Sacrament (see John 3:1–21 and Luther's explanation to the Third Article of the Apostles' Creed in the Small Catechism). We thank God for angels, especially those who safeguard us and our congregations. However, we base our faith on the life, death, and resurrection of our Lord Jesus Christ, in whom alone we have the victory.

John's Revelation probably occurred during the reign of the Roman Emperor Domitian, who presided over a great persecution of the church, one of many that Christians would endure before faith in Jesus would be tolerated under the Emperor Constantine. The seven churches to whom letters were addressed were in the same general area of western Asia that is now called Turkey. Each church had problems that were amplified by persecution. And each church had something for which it could be commended—all but Laodicea, that is.

The medieval church spoke of the seven deadly sins. Traditionally, these were pride, covetousness, lust, envy, gluttony, anger, and sloth. These sins turn one away from God and place the focus on oneself, one's own feelings, and one's own desires. Yet as John witnesses, the sins plaguing the seven churches posed a more deadly and immediate danger because forsaking Christ in favor of idolatry is the root of other sins. For example, gluttony is more than overeating at the family gathering. It is a habit, an enduring decision to make a god out of one's stomach (see Romans 16). Behind the sin of gluttony lies the more fundamental sin of seeking another god. Thus we might call John's concerns for the seven churches the "seven 'deadlier' sins."

Because the churches were so close together geographically and because each letter ends with "hear what the Spirit says to the churches," we can assume that each church was encouraged to read the sacred mail sent to the other churches. Moreover, though the issues addressed are rooted in historical circumstances, they are timeless, relating to Christians in every era, including our own. All churches face the threat of deadly sins such as leaving Christ, their first love; growing fearful of persecution; falling prey to idolatry; succumbing to immorality; and becoming lethargic, neglectful, and complacent. These are not only first-century problems; they are problems in our century as well.

The letters found in Revelation are written for us too. Jesus would have John's letters delivered by angels. Thus in keeping with the spirit of His intent, throughout this Lenten series, the preacher will take the role of angel, perhaps similar to Malachi 2:7. The sermons in this series are written in the first person so worshipers will hear a unique style of delivery during this Lenten season. The names chosen for each angel amplify a specific element of each letter, whether it is a name of Christ or a trait of the particular first-century congregation. Obviously the delivery style and the choice to "name" the angels are matters of personal preference. The sermons may be adapted to reflect the pastor's own style. As pastor and people together visit each of the seven churches, they will hear from the angel what is commended and soberly consider the deadlier sins that are addressed—sins that require repentance and faith in Christ if the hearing congregation is to partake of eternal life. Hear now what the Spirit says to the churches.

SERMON STUDIES

REVELATION 2:1–7

LETTER TO EPHESUS

BACKGROUND

The great unveiling that John experienced occurred while he was in exile on the small, rocky island of Patmos in the Aegean Sea, just off the coast of Asia Minor. The revelation probably occurred between A.D. 81 and A.D. 96, during the reign of the Roman Emperor Domitian. A Greek Orthodox monastery is located on the island today, and tourists may view a hillside grotto, which is the traditional site of Christ's revelation to John.

In Revelation 1:10 and Revelation 1:13, one like a "son of man" appears to John while he is "in the Spirit" on "the Lord's Day," that is, on Sunday, which is the Christian's little Easter. Clearly, "son of man" intentionally recalls the use of the phrase in Daniel 7:13–14 in which the son of man is a messianic figure. Thus John wants his readers to understand that the son of man in his vision is the Messiah, the risen and glorified Jesus. It is this Jesus who instructs John to write letters to the angels of seven mainland churches not far from Patmos.

The word *angel* means "messenger" and can refer to a heavenly being created by God to serve His people (Hebrews 1:14) or to a pastor who brings God's message to the congregation. Because angels in the heavenly sense are so prominent in Revelation, this is probably what John has in mind.

Ephesus is the city nearest Patmos in the clockwise circuit of seven cities to which the letters are addressed. It was a provincial capital, a port city, and the site of one of the seven wonders of the ancient world—the Temple of Artemis, whose image supposedly fell from the sky. (Perhaps her image was crafted from a meteorite and the memory of this was simply lost.) Paul labored in Ephesus, beginning the church there. A riot occurred in this city when silversmiths who made idols of Artemis began losing business because of the growing influence of Christianity (see Acts 19:23–41).

In A.D. 431, the third General Council of the Church met in Ephesus and condemned Nestorianism, the name given to the false doctrine that claimed the two natures in Christ, divine and human, remain separate from each other. The distinction between the two natures does not cease with the union in Christ; both natures retain their respective attributes. Yet Christ is not two persons but one. The natures are not confused with each other, as with the false statement "Man created the world." The natures do not flow together to form a third substance because God, who is one, would then be divided against Himself. The natures may neither be divided nor separated from the union in Christ. God is three persons in one nature and Christ is one person in two natures, fully human and fully divine.

TEXT OUTLINE: EPHESUS (REVELATION 2:1–7)

Destination—"to the angel of the church in Ephesus" (2:1a)

Exaltation—from "Him who holds the seven stars in His right hand and walks among the seven golden lampstands" (2:1b)

Observation—(of the church at Ephesus)

    Commendation—for deeds, hard work, perseverance, intolerance of wicked men, tests of those who claim apostleship, endurance of hardship for Christ's name without growing weary (2:2–3), hatred of the practices of the Nicolaitans (2:6)

    Condemnation—"forsaken your first love" (2:4)

Exhortation—"Remember the height from which you have fallen . . . do the things you did at first" (2:5a)

Notification—"[or] I will come to you and remove your lampstand" (2:5b)

Conclusion

    Formulation—"He who has an ear, let him hear what the Spirit says to the churches" (2:7a)

    Declaration of Salvation—"To him who overcomes, I will give the right to eat from the tree of life, which is in the paradise of God" (2:7b)

COMMENTARY

Verse 1: The letter is addressed to the angel, or messenger, of the church at Ephesus. This could be a heavenly being or the pastor. Both could serve as a spiritual messenger (ἄγγελος). The "seven stars" of Revelation 1:20 are synonymous with the "angels of the seven churches." The "seven golden lampstands" are the "seven churches." Christ's "right hand," the hand of honor, holds the seven stars. Thus the angels of the seven churches are highly honored by Christ. Christ Himself is the one walking amid the seven lampstands. Although unseen, His presence is active, real, and intimate. The lampstands are made of gold; thus they are precious, implying that each church is of great value to Christ. To be a light of Christ's truth is the function of each church. Jesus speaks of John the Baptist in this way: "John was a lamp that burned and gave light, and you chose for a time to enjoy his light" (John 5:35).

Verses 2–3: Christ commends the church at Ephesus for six things: (1) deeds; (2) hard work; (3) perseverance; (4) shunning of wicked men; (5) tests of those who claim apostleship, and (6) the endurance of hardship for Christ's name without growing weary. A seventh commendation appears in verse 6: "You hate the practices of the Nicolaitans."

Verse 2: The Greek word for perseverance, ὑπομονήν, indicates that the congregation holds up under tremendous persecution, suffering patiently. But the congregation is not merely passive. It labors in Christ's cause to the point of weariness. Wicked men are not tolerated. The immoral behavior of wicked men may be meant, but more likely it is the lies they tell, probably their denial that salvation is by God's grace through faith in Christ. Perhaps it is these same wicked men who reject Christ's true apostles, such as Paul, who organized the church, and John, whose home congregation was now Ephesus. Through the congregation's diligence, pretenders claiming to be apostles have been detected and exposed. The Ephesians are reminiscent of the Bereans (Acts 17:11) who searched the Scriptures to see whether Paul's preaching was true. The presence of false apostles fulfills Paul's prophecy in Acts 20:29: "I know that after I leave, savage wolves will come in among you and will not spare the flock."

Verse 3: Despite persecution, the church at Ephesus has endured patiently, continuing to labor in the name of Christ, showing no signs of weariness.

Verse 4: Although characterized by many laudable attributes, Christ is displeased: "I hold [something] against you." Thus it is patently evident that virtue and good works do not save or gain favor with God. The Ephesian Christians have "left" their first love. The stronger word *abandoned* is preferred. In the fray of doctrinal and moral battle, the focus of the Ephesian Christians is no longer Christ's love (ἀγάπη) for them or theirs for Him and for one another. The battle itself has taken first place.

Verse 5: Having left their first love, the Ephesians are called to remember the high position they have in Christ but from which they have fallen. With repentance, they can return to their place of honor among the other lamp-stands, or they can lie dead and in ruins, awaiting removal when Christ comes (damnation?). Merely feeling sorry for sin is not the required repentance. Only a complete change of mind, feeling, and practice will be accepted. For the Ephesians, this would mean turning from self-righteousness and trusting in Christ alone and in His righteousness. Clearly, while Christ says the "gates of Hades" will not prevail against His church (Matthew 16:18), He does not mean an individual congregation can expect to exist indefinitely apart from faith and repentance.

Verse 6: Oddly, the final commendation of the congregation occurs after the most dire of warnings. Both the Ephesian church and Christ hate the works of the Nicolaitans. Mentioned here and in verse 15, the Nicolaitans probably tried to mix (syncretize) idolatry and sexual immorality with Christian faith and practice. Irenaeus says the leader of this movement was Nicolas, one of the seven chosen in Acts 6:5 to help the apostles, but there is no evidence of this. The Ephesians will not tolerate the practices of the Nicolaitans. Neither will Christ. Note that while love may be the chief attribute of the Christian, it is not wrong to hate evil.

Verse 7: "He who has an ear, let him hear" is the formula that concludes each letter to the Asian churches. To "hear" means more than to recognize the meaning of Christ's words. Rather, it means to believe and to act on them. For the Ephesians, doing so gains the promise of eating "from the tree of life, which is in the paradise of God." For those whose first love is Christ, Adam's curse is cancelled, replaced by an invitation to return to the garden and enjoy eternal life.

Sermon Outline Suggestion

Come! Eat from the tree!

Goal—Jesus invites us to a feast from the tree of life.

Malady—Enemies of faith threaten to block our way to the feast from the tree of life.

Means—By the Spirit, through the Word, we overcome every enemy and enjoy the feast from the tree of life.

REVELATION 2:8–11

LETTER TO SMYRNA

BACKGROUND

Smyrna is modern-day Izmir and was about forty miles north of Ephesus in this group of seven churches. A wealthy and beautiful seaport, Smyrna was considered the "crown" of Asia and featured a library, stadium, theater, and temples. The word *crown* in Revelation 2:10 may allude to Smyrna's fame as a site for athletic games because winners received a garland.

Destroyed in 580 B.C., Smyrna was rebuilt in 290 B.C. according to a comprehensive plan. The city's rebirth may suggest Christ's resurrection because He "died and came to life again" (Revelation 2:8b). An early and voluntary ally of Rome, Smyrna had temples to the goddess Rome, the Emperor Tiberius, and the Roman senate.

Christians in Smyrna faced the hostility of pagans and of a large Jewish community. Polycarp, bishop of Smyrna, was born about A.D. 69 and may have known the apostle John, whose writing he quotes. A defender of orthodoxy, Polycarp was martyred about A.D. 155 for refusing to deny his faith in Christ.

Interestingly, the letter to Smyrna contains no specific criticism or warning.

TEXT OUTLINE: SMYRNA (REVELATION 2:8–11)

Destination—"to the angel of the church in Smyrna" (2:8a)

Exaltation—"of Him who is the First and the Last, who died and came to life again" (2:8b)

Observation—(of the church at Smyrna)

    Commendation—despite affliction and poverty, the church is rich, endurance of slander (2:9)

    Condemnation—(There is none.)

Exhortation—"Do not be afraid" (2:10a), "be faithful" (2:10c)

Notification—"You are about to suffer . . . the devil will put some of you in prison . . . you will suffer persecution for ten days" (2:10b)

Conclusion

    Formulation—"He who has an ear, let him hear what the Spirit says to the churches" (2:11a)

    Declaration of Salvation—"He who overcomes will not be hurt at all by the second death" (2:11b)

COMMENTARY

Verse 8: Note the formula that is repeated at the beginning of this and the other letters: "To the angel of the church in . . . ." This opening is followed by "these are the words of . . . ." In the formula, the church addressed is identified and some truth about Christ is stated. The words of this letter come from "Him who is the First and the Last [πρῶτος καὶ ὁ ἔσχατος], who died and came to life again." "First and last" is also used of Christ in Revelation 1:17, and Revelation 22:13 and is similar to the title "Alpha and Omega," which is ascribed to God in Revelation 1:8. Christ is the beginning and ending of everything. He is eternal and all encompassing. Thus identified, Christ's major work is presented: He died and came to life, giving Him the right to bestow eternal life on all who have faith.

Verse 9: As the eternal, saving God, Christ knows the crushing afflictions endured by the church at Smyrna. Yet His knowledge is also the intimate knowledge of a human being who has experienced the same thing: "I've been there, too, and feel what you do." It is likely that the congregation's extreme poverty is linked to the affliction of persecution. As members of an illegal religion, Christians in Smyrna may have faced barriers to employment and trade. Such barriers may have been put in place by Jewish opponents whose religion was legal. Despite material poverty, the Christians are "rich" with the blessings given to the true children of God who have the forgiveness of sins and the hope of heaven. The Jews in Smyrna, on the other hand, are called "a synagogue of Satan," recalling Christ's condemnation of His enemies in John 8:44a: "You belong to your father, the devil." The allegations of the Jews denied that Jesus is the Son of God.

Verse 10: Current suffering is only the beginning for the church in Smyrna; yet to come is prison. Although the suffering will be intense, it will be limited to "ten days." This is not to be understood literally but figuratively as a limited period with a definite end. The conclusion of suffering could be the moment persecution ceases or it could be when the persecuted

Christian dies and receives "the crown of life" in heaven. Either way, this crown (στέφανος, the victor's wreath) awaits the faithful.

Verse 11: The usual closing formula is given but with the promise that "he who overcomes will not be hurt at all by the second death." Also mentioned in Revelation 20:6, Revelation 20:14, and Revelation 21:8, the second death is eternal punishment, the antithesis of eternal life. The use of the double negative, οὐ μὴ ("no, not ever"), reinforces this promise. He who overcomes will by no means be hurt by the second death.

SERMON OUTLINE SUGGESTION

Come! Take your crown!

Goal—A crown of life won by Jesus awaits us.

Malady—Many frightening things stand between us and the crown of life.

Means—Because Jesus died and lives again, our crown of life is certain.

REVELATION 2:12–17

LETTER TO PERGAMUM

BACKGROUND

Ancient Pergamum (which means "fortress" or "citadel") is modern-day Bergama, Turkey. Pergamum was located 50 miles north of ancient Smyrna and 15 miles from the Aegean Sea. It was built atop a 1,000-foot high hill. Pergamum was willed to Rome by its last king in 133 B.C. By the second century after Christ's birth, Pergamum was a center of art, culture, and religion. In fact, parchment was developed here as a substitute for papyrus, and the city's library held 200,000 parchment scrolls.

A great altar to Zeus was located in Pergamum, as well as temples that honored Dionysus and Athena, the city's patron goddess. A temple to Asclepius, the Greek god of healing, whose image was a serpent, made Pergamum the pagan equivalent of Lourdes. "Satan's throne" (Revelation 2:13) may be a reference to the city's prominence as the chief center of the imperial cult in this part of the world (Pergamum featured three temples dedicated to the emperor) or to the overwhelmingly pagan character of the city.

Antipas, the faithful martyr, is unknown apart from the reference in Revelation 2:13.

TEXT OUTLINE: PERGAMUM (REVELATION 2:12–17)

Destination—"to the angel of the church in Pergamum" (2:12a)
Exaltation—"of Him who has the sharp, double-edged sword" (2:12b)
Observation—(of the church at Pergamum)
   Commendation—"for living within Satan's sphere yet remaining true to Christ's name, for not renouncing the faith" (2:13)
   Condemnation—some hold to "the teaching of Balaam" and the Nicolaitans (2:14–15) (both attempt to combine idolatrous practices with sexual immorality)
Exhortation—"Repent" (2:16a)

Notification—"Otherwise, I will soon come to you and will fight against them with the sword of My mouth" (2:16)

Conclusion

Formulation—"He who has an ear, let him hear what the Spirit says to the churches" (2:17a)

Declaration of Salvation—"To him who overcomes, I will give some of the hidden manna. I will also give him a white stone with a new name written on it" (2:17b)

COMMENTARY

Verse 12: The greeting describes the divine author of the letter as possessing "the sharp, double-edged sword." In Revelation 1:16, the sword is pictured as coming out of the son of man's mouth. In Revelation 2:16, the sword threatens those who hold to the doctrine of the Nicolaitans. While a sword may threaten an attack, it also can defend. Because it comes from the mouth of the son of man, the sword is understood as the Word of God, which contains both Law and Gospel. This Word threatens the unrepentant but defends the faithful.

Verse 13: In His omniscience, Christ the sword-bearer knows all about the Christians at Pergamum. Despite the pervasive influence of paganism—Satan's throne is there—the church holds fast to the name of Christ, refusing to renounce it. The mention of Satan's throne perhaps alludes to the temple to Asclepius whose image was a serpent. In Judeo-Christian metaphor, the serpent is an incarnation of Satan (Genesis 3:1). "Even in the days of Antipas" indicates that though persecution had been intense, the Christians still did not renounce Christ. Antipas is otherwise unknown, though legend says he was roasted in a bronze bowl. "Martyr" (μάρτυς) literally means "witness," but those who were witnesses to Christ were persecuted and killed so often that the word came to mean "one who dies for Christ."

Verse 14: As with the church at Ephesus, so the church at Pergamum can take no confidence in its good works. Despite its faithful adherence to the name of Christ, some hold to the false teaching of Balaam. The reference is to the pseudo-prophet Balaam (Numbers 22:1–24:25; 31:1–16) who was hired by Balak, king of Moab, to curse Israel. Prevented from doing so, Balaam conspired with Balak to seduce the men of Israel to commit acts of sexual immorality with pagan Moabite women. The effect of false teachers in Pergamum is the same: The faithful will not renounce Christ, but they can be seduced in more subtle ways. This becomes a stumbling block (σκάνδαλον).

Verse 15: Also among the Christians at Pergamum are those who adhere to the equally destructive doctrine of the Nicolaitans. According to Leon Morris, Victorinus of Pettau, the first commentator on Revelation, claims that the Nicolaitans advocated eating meat sacrificed to idols and promised peace to fornicators on the eighth day after the offense. Thus the Balaamites and Nicolaitans are not identical, but both are corrosive to saving faith and right living.

Verse 16: The command to repent is sharp and comes from Christ Himself. But note that Christ will "come to you" but will "fight against them" with the sword of His mouth. Thus it is not the entire congregation that is infected with the disease, only some members.

Verse 17: The familiar concluding formula closes with somewhat obscure promises. Perhaps the manna that has been hidden is spiritual food, unrecognized by the world but seen and enjoyed by those of faith. The white stone has many interpretations. The best might be the Greek practice of giving jurors a black stone and a white stone. Casting the black stone meant guilt; the white one meant acquittal. The new name on the white stone may be symbolic of the new person a penitent becomes by faith in Christ.

Sermon Outline Suggestion

Come! Enjoy the manna!

Goal—Jesus promises hidden manna to those who overcome.

Malady—Sometimes it seems more likely that temptations will overcome us than that we will overcome temptations.

Means—The sword of Christ's word defeats temptations and protects believers, empowering us to overcome and to enjoy the hidden manna.

REVELATION 2:18–29

LETTER TO THYATIRA

BACKGROUND

Thyatira is the smallest and least important town of the seven that received correspondence from John, yet its church receives the longest letter. Founded by the Macedonians, Thyatira was located about 30 miles southeast of Pergamum on the Lycus River. The modern-day town is Ak-Hissar.

Thyatira was not important for art or culture but as a commercial center. Inscriptions mention wool; linen- and leatherworkers; tanners, dyers and garment makers; potters; bakers; slave traders; and bronzesmiths. Lydia, one of Paul's converts in Philippi, was a dealer in purple cloth from Thyatira (Acts 16:13–15).

By the third century after Christ's birth, Thyatira was a stronghold of Montanism, a heretical sect known for its strict asceticism and manifestations of the Holy Spirit through prophets and prophetesses. Perhaps this was in reaction to the religious and moral laxity mentioned in the letter.

TEXT OUTLINE: THYATIRA (REVELATION 2:18–29)

Destination—"to the angel of the church in Thyatira" (2:18a)

Exaltation—"of the Son of God, whose eyes are like blazing fire and whose feet are like burnished bronze" (2:18b)

Observation—(of the church at Thyatira)

Commendation—"I know your deeds, your love and faith, your service and perseverance, and that you are now doing more than you did at first" (2:19)

Condemnation—"You tolerate . . . Jezebel, who calls herself a prophetess [and leads] My servants into sexual immorality and the eating of food sacrificed to idols" (2:20)

Exhortation—Repent (2: 21–22), "hold on to what you have until I come" (2:25)

Notification—"I will cast her [and those who commit adultery with her] on a bed of suffering . . . I will strike her children dead. Then all the churches will know that I am He who searches hearts and minds, and I will repay each of you according to your deeds" (2:22–23)

Conclusion

Declaration of Salvation—"To him who overcomes and does My will to the end, I will give authority over the nations [to participate in their judgment] . . . . I will also give him the morning star" (2:26–28)

Formulation—"He who has an ear, let him hear what the Spirit says to the churches" (2:29)

COMMENTARY

Verse 18: In Revelation 1:13–15, Christ is identified as one like a son of man. Here, He is described in similar words but called "the Son of God."

Verse 19: The Christians at Thyatira are more virtuous than those in the church at Ephesus (Revelation 2:2). They are characterized by works, love, faith, service, and endurance. In fact, they do more now than they did at first.

Verse 20: Just like the Christians at Ephesus and Pergamum, the Christians at Thyatira, Christ's "slaves," tolerate Jezebel's deceptive teaching and practice. From the description of her errors—seducing Christians into committing fornication and eating meat sacrificed to idols—Jezebel's misdeeds are similar to those of the Balaamites and the Nicolaitans.

Verse 21: The patience of Christ is exhibited as He grants Jezebel time to repent, but she is "unwilling."

Verse 22: The punishment of this Jezebel is even now in effect. The bed of terrible affliction she is cast on may be the logical and biological consequences of sin. But one also wonders if this is related to an unworthy reception of Christ's body and blood in the Lord's Supper (1 Corinthians 11:28–31) or a refusal to confess sin (James 5:14–16).

Verse 23: Those Jezebel has seduced into her error share the same fate—death (eternal?)—if they do not repent. Christ's dreadful judgment is not only retributive but also preventative. As the churches observe the terrible fate of Jezebel and her followers, they know their own hearts and minds ("kidneys," νεφρούς, used metaphorically) are open to the Lord's scrutiny. They, too, will be dealt with according to their works. Those of true faith will demonstrate it and not join Jezebel and her ilk.

Verses 24–25: Mention of the knowledge of the deep things of Satan may harbor sarcasm. Whatever knowledge false teachers such as Jezebel, the

Nicolaitans, and the Balaamites claim to have is nothing but the lies of the devil. Those who have not succumbed to the deception—the faithful in Thyatira—are not burdened with anything but are called to remain faithful, to hold fast to the truth until Jesus comes. Such a charge is no burden at all.

Verse 26: The usual "he who overcomes" includes a new element: "[he who] does My will to the end." Such an individual has the promise of being given authority over the nations, that is, reigning with Christ in glory.

Verse 27: An ominous note of retributive justice is spoken: "He will rule them with an iron scepter; He will dash them to pieces like pottery." That Jesus is the Son of God is clear from His words "just as I have received authority from My Father."

Verse 28: The promise of the morning star is doubtless the promise of seeing Christ and being in His presence eternally (see Revelation 22:16).

Verse 29: Note that it is not only Thyatira that needs to hear these words but also "the churches." The churches are all those called out and gathered from the world by the Gospel.

SERMON OUTLINE SUGGESTION

Come! Reach the star!

Goal—Being with Jesus, the Morning Star, is the sure hope of every Christian.

Malady—When evil is pervasive, being with Jesus, the Morning Star, can seem impossible.

Means—The Word that brought us to faith is what draws us back to faith, assuring us that we will indeed overcome and be with Jesus, the Morning Star.

REVELATION 3:1–6

LETTER TO SARDIS

BACKGROUND

Sardis was located 30 miles southeast of Thyatira in the circuit of seven churches to which John wrote. Dating from the beginning of the Iron Age, Sardis was well suited for commerce because it was situated on an east-west road. The capital of wealthy Lydia, Sardis manufactured textiles, jewelry, and perhaps the world's first coins, which were produced during the reign of Croesus.

Although built on a steep hill and fortified with what were thought to be impregnable defenses, Cyrus the Great conquered Sardis in the sixth century before Christ. Antiochus the Great conquered it in the third century before Christ. Both times the attackers scaled the walls at night, undetected by watchmen who were perhaps sleeping.

Sardis was destroyed by an earthquake in A.D. 17, profoundly affecting the overconfident citizens. It was rebuilt with generous aid from the Emperor Tiberius. Mystery cults flourished in Sardis, especially worship of Cybele, goddess of the fruitful earth.

TEXT OUTLINE: SARDIS (REVELATION 3:1–6)

Destination—"to the angel of the church in Sardis" (3:1a)
Exaltation—"of Him who holds the seven spirits of God and the seven stars" (3:1b)
Observation—(of the church at Sardis)
   Commendation—"a few people in Sardis . . . have not soiled their clothes" (3:4 only)
   Condemnation—"you have a reputation of being alive, but you are dead" (3:1b), the deeds of the Sardis Christians are incomplete (3:2b)
Exhortation—"Wake up! Strengthen what remains . . . Remember . . . what you have received and heard . . . obey it, and repent" (3:2–3a)
Notification—"If you do not wake up, I will come like a thief" (3:3b)
Conclusion

Declaration of Salvation—those who have not soiled their clothes "will walk with Me, dressed in white" (3:4b); "he who overcomes will . . . be dressed in white. I will never blot out his name from the book of life, but will acknowledge his name before My Father and His angels" (3:5) Formulation—"He who has an ear, let him hear what the Spirit says to the churches" (3:6)

COMMENTARY

Verse 1: The "seven Spirits of God" is not literal but describes the one Spirit's complete perfection. The use of the number seven may recall the seven attributes of the Spirit listed in Isaiah 11:2. There He is "the Spirit of the LORD" (who rests on Christ, the shoot that comes up from the stump of Jesse), "the Spirit of wisdom and of understanding, the Spirit of counsel and of power, the Spirit of knowledge and of the fear of the LORD." The seven stars already have been identified in Revelation 1:20 as the seven angels of the seven churches, either the pastors or spiritual messengers. Christ, the speaker, knows the works of the people in the Sardis congregation, and He knows they have made a name (ὄνομα) for themselves as a living congregation, but the truth is the people of the congregation are dead.

Verse 2: Sardis is admonished to "be watching" (present participle)— not to "wake up" as the New International Version translates it—or what remains will die. Although appearing to be a threat, this is in fact good news. Something of the true faith remains at Sardis. All is not yet lost. Nevertheless, the works of the church at Sardis are incomplete, unperfected before "My God," as Jesus speaks of the Father.

Verse 3: *Remember* (μνημόνευε) is a present imperative and means to "keep in mind," not just "recall." The congregation's members are to bear in mind the manner in which they heard the Gospel. We wonder what special circumstances accompanied their initial hearing and believing. Whatever the manner, the Christians in Sardis are to hold fast and repent. If not, Christ will come as a thief. He will come anyway, a joyful hope for the faithful, but for the unwatchful, Christ's arrival will be unexpected and have negative consequences.

Verses 4–5: Other good news for Sardis, besides the fact that all has not yet been lost, is that Christ knows the names of some who have not defiled their clothes (likely by participating in the orgiastic rites associated with worship of Cybele). Four promises are made to the undefiled Christians: (1) They will walk with Christ dressed in white. (2) Those who overcome also will be dressed in white (perhaps referring to the unwatchful who eventually heed the warning and repent). (3) Their names will not be blotted out of the Book of Life. (4) Christ will confess their names before His Father and the angels. All this seems to be an assurance that those of faith who demonstrate it by their watchfulness are justified, that is, forgiven, declared righteous (thus the white clothing), and have a home in heaven. The faithful have nothing to fear, for they will find Christ is faithful to them.

Verse 6: The usual formula concludes the letter.

Sermon Outline Suggestion

Come! Wear your dress whites!

Goal—Put on your dress whites and celebrate your righteousness.

Malady—Sin makes us unrighteous, so how can we put on our dress whites and celebrate?

Means—Our righteousness comes not from ourselves but from Christ who died for us and who clothes us with His righteousness as a gift of faith.

REVELATION 3:7–13

LETTER TO PHILADELPHIA

BACKGROUND

Founded in 140 B.C., Philadelphia, which means "brotherly love," was a gateway to the east. It was located 30 miles southeast of Sardis at the junction of three important roads. The name commemorates the loyalty of Attalus II of Pergamum to his brother Eumenes II. Attalus intended the city to promote the Hellenistic way of life. It was a center for the cult of Dionysus, but temples to other gods also existed. A staple of the economy was grape cultivation. Ala-Sheher, the modern name, means "city of God."

The sixth church of the seven to receive letters, Philadelphia had seen its share of catastrophic earthquakes. Pillars in the pagan temples had no doubt fallen, something that, according to Revelation 3:12, will not happen to faithful Christians who become pillars in the temple of God. As with the church at Smyrna, there is no explicit criticism. Enemies of the church appear to come from without, not within.

Philadelphia's Greco-Roman culture endured until 1390 when the city fell to Bajazet I. Ruins of many ancient churches can be seen in this area.

TEXT OUTLINE: PHILADELPHIA (REVELATION 3:7–13)

Destination—"to the angel of the church in Philadelphia" (3:7a)
Exaltation—"of Him who is holy and true, who holds the key of David. What He opens no one can shut, and what He shuts no one can open" (3:7b). According to commentator Louis Brighton, this could suggest opportunities to serve the Lord and His people through proclamation of the Gospel (see 1 Corinthians 16:8–9, which mentions "a great door for effective work" that the people were not fully using).
Observation—(of the church at Philadelphia)
Commendation—for deeds; despite little strength, the Christians of Philadelphia have Christ's word, not denied His name (3:8), and kept His command to endure patiently (3:10a)
Condemnation—(There is none.)

Notification—to those who are a synagogue of Satan, falsely claiming to be
Jews: "I will make them come and fall down at your feet and acknowledge
that I have loved you" (3:9)

Exhortation—"Hold on to what you have" (3:11a)

Conclusion

Declaration of Salvation—to those who endure patiently: "I will also
keep you from the hour of trial" (3:10b); "no one will take your crown"
(3:11b); and "him who overcomes I will make a pillar in the temple of
My God . . . the names of My God and the name of the city of My God,
the new Jerusalem . . . and I will also write on him My new name" (3:12)

Formulation—"He who has an ear, let him hear what the Spirit says to
the churches" (3:13)

COMMENTARY

Verse 7: After the opening formula, Christ cites credentials that affirm
His complete trustworthiness. He is "holy and true." As David's descendant, Christ has the "key of David," the legitimate authority to open and
shut the kingdom of God to whomever He will. Perhaps this is said to reassure those who are being threatened by non-Christian Jews who would
deny believing Gentiles a place in God's kingdom. We might identify the
keys as those Jesus gives to the church as she confesses Him to be "the
Christ, the Son of the Living God" (Matthew 16:16).

Verse 8: As Christ says of Ephesus, Thyatira, Sardis, and Laodicea, so He
says of Philadelphia: "I know your deeds." Just what these deeds are is not
specified, but perhaps they have kept Christ's word, not denied His name,
and patiently endured (3:8, 10). "I have placed before you an open door that
no one can shut." This appears to be a digression from the main thought
that Christ knows the deeds of the Philadelphian Christians and that
though they have only a little power, they kept Christ's word and refused to
deny His name.

Verse 9: Christ would have us "see" (3:8) that is, "behold," what He gives
the synagogue of Satan. The members of this synagogue are those who
falsely claim to be Jews (see Revelation 2:9). John would have us realize that
no true Jew would deny that Jesus is the Christ. According to St. Paul in
Romans 4:16, all who are of faith in Christ are the real children of Abraham, including Jews and Gentiles. So what is it that Christ gives this synagogue of Satan? "[They] will . . . come and fall down at your feet," that is,

they will humbly acknowledge the faithful Christians in Philadelphia by falling down and kissing their feet. By so doing, they acknowledge these Christians as the true Jews, loved by Christ. This may occur on the Day of Judgment.

Verse 10: Having faithfully endured and kept His word, Christ promises that the Christians in Philadelphia will be kept from the hour of trial about to come on the household of earth. It should be noted that this does not require a pretribulational rapture. Being "kept from" refers to an individual's security in Christ amid trials, not necessarily being taken out of them. Whatever the trial, it is limited, lasting only one hour, and the believer is safe.

Verse 11: Christ's coming is a recurring thought in the letters to the seven churches. See Revelation 2:5, 16, 25; 3:3, 11. So also is the imperative to "hold on to what you have" (κράτει ὃ ἔχεις) in view of Christ's coming (Revelation 2:25; 3:3, 11). Holding on assures believers that no one will take their crown, which is the victor's garland referred to in Revelation 2:10.

Verse 12: The repetitive closing formula includes the promise that the one who overcomes (ὁ νικῶν, present active participle derived from νική, "victory") will be made a pillar in the temple, a position from which he can never be removed. God's name, the name of the city of God, the new Jerusalem, and Christ's new name are written on the one who overcomes, identifying him as God's possession, a citizen of the kingdom of God. Christ's new name may allude to the consummation of history when all the world bows the knee in recognition that Jesus Christ is Lord (see Philippians 2:10–11).

Verse 13: The concluding formula occurs without variation.

SERMON OUTLINE SUGGESTION

Come! Get a new name!
Goal—In Christ, every believer has a new start and a new name.
Malady—Because of sin, we may think we have lost our new name.
Means—Christ's word, received in repentance and faith, not our behavior guarantees our new name, now and in eternity.

REVELATION 3:14–22

LETTER TO LAODICEA

BACKGROUND

Laodicea lay in the valley at the junction of the Lycus and Maeander Rivers and at the intersection of three major roads. Five of the seven churches in Revelation were located on one of these roads. The gateway to Phrygia, Laodicea had grown wealthy from banking, clothing manufacture, and black wool cloth. The modern name of the ancient town is Eski-hisar.

A god of healing, Men Carou, was the city's patron deity. Laodicea's medical school and eye and ear ointments were famous. There also was a thriving emperor cult, yet thousands of Jews freely practiced their religion in Laodicea.

Epaphras may have started the church in Laodicea (see Colossians 1:7). A letter from Paul to the Laodiceans has been lost (see Colossians 4:16).

TEXT OUTLINE: LAODICEA (REVELATION 3:14–22)

Destination—"to the angel of the church in Laodicea" (3:14a)

Exaltation—"[of Him who is] the Amen, the faithful and true witness, the ruler of God's creation" (3:14b)

Observation—(of the church at Laodicea)

    Commendation—(There is none.)

    Condemnation—"you are neither cold nor hot . . . [but] lukewarm" (3:15); despite claims of wealth and lacking nothing, the Laodician Christians "are wretched, pitiful, poor, blind and naked" (3:17)

Notification—"Because you are lukewarm—neither hot not cold—I am about to spit you out of My mouth" (3:16); "those whom I love I rebuke and discipline" (3:19a)

Exhortation—"Buy from Me gold refined in the fire . . . and white clothes . . . [to] cover your shameful nakedness; and salve to put on your eyes, so you can see" (3:18); "be earnest and repent" (3:19b)

Conclusion

    Declaration of Salvation—"I stand at the door and knock. If anyone hears My voice and opens the door, I will come in and eat with him, and he with Me" (3:20); "to him who overcomes, I will give the right to sit with Me on My throne" (3:21)

Formulation—"He who has an ear, let him hear what the Spirit says to the churches" (3:22)

COMMENTARY

Verse 14: The opening formula identifies the author as the "faithful and true witness," which hearkens back to Revelation 1:5. In both passages, Christ can be thought of as "the faithful martyr" because of His death and resurrection, the ultimate witness of His glory. He is also the "Amen," a Hebrew term used to identify God in Isaiah 65:16 ("the God of Amen"), though English translations have "the God of truth." All these terms describe Christ as faithful and true in all things, which offers a sharp contrast to the enemies of the truth, both within and without the church. Additionally, Christ is ἡ ἀρχὴ τῆς κτίσεως τοῦ θεοῦ, "the ruler ["chief" or "beginning"] of the creation of God." While the Arian heretics of old might have used this to claim that Christ is the first and highest of all creation, Paul affirms that all things were created by and for Christ (Colossians 1:16).

Verses 15–16: Again, Christ is fully aware of the works of each congregation: "I know your deeds." In the case of Laodicea, the congregation is not admonished for idolatry, syncretism, immorality, or tolerating the same but for being neither cold nor hot. Instead, the Christians of Laodicea are lukewarm, a noxious sensation that causes the contents to be vomited out of the mouth. The verb is present active indicative, thus indicating an immediate and present spiritual danger in which the complacent Laodiceans have placed themselves.

Verse 17: The indifference of the Laodiceans to the grace of God in Christ is manifested in their sense of self-sufficiency: "I am rich; I have acquired wealth." Perhaps this redundancy could be paraphrased as "I have become richer than rich." Multiplying the redundancy is the claim of not needing anything. An awakening is needed, and it comes in the words of Christ: "You do not realize that you are wretched, pitiful, poor, blind and naked." Despite their great wealth, enviable medical care, and the finest clothing available, the congregation at Laodicea is a sorry lot of helpless, needy sinners.

Verse 18: But the Laodiceans need not stay that way. Christ invites them to buy refined gold, white clothing (in contrast to the local black wool), and eye salve. All these things can only refer to spiritual blessings: the riches of forgiveness in the Gospel, the righteousness of Christ that clothes the sinner in Baptism, and the ability to apprehend the truth of Christ (see John 9:35–41; Galatians 3:27; Ephesians 1:7–8). The Laodiceans are more than eager to buy fine things. But it is ironic that the rich things Christ urges them to "buy" from Him will cost nothing because He has paid the price on Calvary's cross (see Isaiah 52:1–3; 55:1–2).

Verse 19: Despite the harsh sounding words in Revelation 3:16, the complacent Laodiceans are still the objects of Christ's love: "Those whom I love I rebuke and discipline." Christ's goal is never to vomit out one whom He loves as His own brother. Rather, He wants them to repent, to change their minds and direction, and to be hot or, as some might say, "to be on fire for the Lord." In fact, Christ wants all the blessings of Revelation 3:18 for those He loves.

Verse 20: This verse is used by some evangelists to urge lost sinners to "open the door," promising that if they do, Christ will "come in." However, the verse is not directed at the lost but at lukewarm church members who are loved by Christ. They already are justified by grace through faith and need only to hear the admonishment of the one who has saved them. Intimate fellowship (at the Lord's Table?) is restored when they do.

Verses 21–22: Christ overcame sin, death, and the devil by way of the cross. Joined to Christ and His victory by faith, the Christian overcomes the temptations of wealth, self-sufficiency, and complacency and sits with Christ on the Father's throne. The highest honor imaginable awaits the one who "has an ear" and hears "what the Spirit says to the churches."

SERMON OUTLINE SUGGESTION

Come! Sit on a throne!

Goal—The only throne that matters is the one believers sit on with Christ.

Malady—Prosperity and good health can prevent us from seeing the great value of our promised throne.

Means—God's Word rebukes us, bringing us back to Christ, who stands at the door and knocks, calling us to His Supper and to His throne.

SOURCES

Aland, K., M. Black, C. Martini, B. Metzger, and A. Wikgren, editors. *The Greek New Testament.* 2nd edition. Wuerttemberg: United Bible Societies, 1968.

Arndt, W. F., and F. W. Gingrich. *A Greek-English Lexicon of the New Testament and Other Early Christian Literature.* Chicago: University of Chicago Press, 1957.

Brighton, Louis. *Revelation.* The Concordia Commentary. St. Louis: Concordia, 1999.

Cross, F. L., and E. A. Livingstone, editors. *The Oxford Dictionary of the Christian Church.* 2nd edition. New York: Oxford University Press, 1983.

Guthrie, Donald, editor. *The New Bible Commentary.* 3rd revised edition. Grand Rapids: Eerdmans, 1970.

Hoerber, Robert G. *The Concordia Self-Study Bible.* St. Louis: Concordia, 1986.

Kautz, Darrel P. *Understanding the Book of Revelation.* Milwaukee: self-published, 1985.

Marshall, A., and J. B. Phillips. *The Interlinear Greek-English New Testament.* The Zondervan Parallel New Testament in Greek and English. Grand Rapids: Zondervan, 1975.

Morris, Leon, and R. V. G. Tasker, editors. *The Revelation of St. John.* The Tyndale New Testament Commentaries 20. Grand Rapids: Eerdmans, 1979.

Moulton, Harold. *The Analytical Greek Lexicon.* Grand Rapids: Zondervan, 1974.

Unger, Merrill F. *Unger's Bible Dictionary.* Chicago: Moody, 1972.

SERMONS AND CHILDREN'S MESSAGES

ASH WEDNESDAY

THE LETTER TO EPHESUS: LOVE LOST, DEATH FOUND

Genesis 3:21–23; Revelation 2:1–7; John 15:9–17

THEME VERSE

I hold this against you: You have forsaken your first love. (Revelation 2:4)

Greetings from John the apostle! He sends his regrets that he can't be with you today, but as you know, he is a prisoner on the island of Patmos, about a hundred miles due south of here. He is deeply concerned for your well-being and faith, surrounded as you are by so much pagan wickedness and so many false teachers who even now are trying to make inroads into your congregation here at Ephesus.

What an amazing man! John is nearly one hundred years old, the last surviving apostle. He can't walk anymore, as you already know from what you have seen. The last time he was with you, he was carried out of the church on a stretcher by his friends. His sermon was short that day, only three words: "Love one another." He spoke these three words repeatedly as he was carried away.

Perhaps I should introduce myself. I'm sure you think me a stranger. You are wondering what right I have to come into your church and speak to you unannounced like this. Let me assure you that though you have never seen me before, I know you well. In fact, I am your angel. No, don't be alarmed! I am not here to frighten you. I'm here to proclaim the Gospel, encourage you in the things you are doing right, and do some prodding in those areas that need improvement. I have been with you all along. You just didn't know it. I serve our common Lord and Master, Jesus Christ, so you might not fall into sin. And you have been keeping me busy!

You can call me Zoe, a name that means "life" in the Greek language. I am here to remind you that life is what God wants for you, eternal life, drinking the living water from the source in Jesus, continuing firm in Christian faith and love. Jesus is the one who commanded the things John wrote, the things He gave to me to share with you. John would much rather be here doing the talking, but the Romans don't give weekend passes to prisoners. So Jesus told John what to write, then said to give the letter to me. And here it is.

First, the good news: You are a remarkable congregation, the oldest and biggest in this part of Asia. This is as it should be because Ephesus is the provincial capital, wealthy and populous. Although your congregation has grown, I am fully aware that your journey in faith has not been easy. Remember your history. The apostle Paul began the work here more than forty years ago. When you met Paul, some of you were still disciples of John the Baptist. You had not yet heard that the Messiah, whose way the Baptist prepared, had come. Eagerly you heard Paul's good news. You were baptized, and the Holy Spirit filled you with His gifts.

For two difficult years Paul labored among you. There was strong opposition from the synagogue, but you honored the name of the Lord Jesus anyway. Miracles of healing were common among you in those early days. There were many who publicly repented of sin. Even sorcerers turned from evil to Christ, burning their scrolls, which were worth thousands of drachmas. In fact, so many people became Christians that the silversmiths who made statues of Artemis, goddess of Ephesus, began to lose business. Few seemed interested in visiting her temple anymore. It was one of the seven wonders of the ancient world, but if Artemis was not a real goddess, who cared? The silversmiths whose livelihood was disappearing felt so threatened that they started a riot. Paul barely escaped with his life. Those were dangerous times for Christians in Ephesus, but you persevered.

Eventually, after suffering persecution in Palestine, the apostle John came to live among you as pastor and bishop. Under John's shepherding you flourished. Now, though he cannot be here with you, he would be pleased to see that you still are an example of good works and faithfulness. Other churches without a pastor might become lazy, neglecting works of charity. They might become morally and doctrinally lax with no one to encourage them, but not you. You have shown yourselves to be different.

Your beloved John, whom I serve, writes these words of Jesus to you: "I know your deeds, your hard work and your perseverance. I know that you cannot tolerate wicked men, that you have tested those who claim to be apostles but are not, and have found them false. You have persevered and have endured hardships for My name, and have not grown weary" (Revelation 2:2–3). Moreover, Jesus says: "You hate the practices of the Nicolaitans, which I also hate" (Revelation 3:6). Those are the people willing to compromise faith for money, people who teach that immorality is okay because grace covers sin. But you know better than to use grace as an excuse to do wrong. History will show that one of your future pastors, Polycrates, will defend the resurrection of Jesus and continue to celebrate it on its exact anniversary each year despite opposition from the pope. Such is the degree of firmness with which you cling to your convictions. Not only are you champions of the apostolic doctrine, you do not hesitate to expose those who would mislead your brothers and sisters in the congregation. Centuries from now, may the faith of this congregation be as steadfast as it is today.

There is only one problem, which may be imperceptible to some but is a creeping cancer that will destroy your church if it is not removed. That is the bad news I bring. Your hard work and good deeds, your doctrinal and moral purity will count for nothing without love for Christ. As His messenger, it is a hard thing I must tell you, but "you have forsaken your first love. Remember the height from which you have fallen! Repent and do the things you did at first. If you do not repent, I [Jesus] will come to you and remove your lampstand from its place" (Revelation 2:4–5).

You seem puzzled. Perhaps you are wondering how I can celebrate what is good in the congregation here at Ephesus then proceed to threaten that God might remove your church. Good works count for nothing without a heart that loves Christ who loves you. "Greater love has no one than this, that he lay down his life for his friends," says Jesus (John 15:13). With His own life's blood, He has poured out His love for you. Oh, the agony of soul and body Christ endured for you in His prayer at Gethsemane, in His trials before priests and politicians, and most of all on His cross. Oh, how He loves you! Now you are saved. Now you are declared innocent in the eyes of the Lord. Now you have been called to be part of God's holy people.

Dear friends, Christ our Lord has loved you with an everlasting love. He has given you faith and filled you with the Holy Spirit. Respond to His love for you with your love for Him. Repent of the coldness of your hearts. As Jesus reminds us: "Love the Lord your God with all your heart and with all your soul and with all your mind. This is the first and greatest commandment" (Matthew 22:37–38).

Christ's love gives life to the Christian. It builds and sustains the church. It is central to everything. Without it, there is no life, only death. There may be zeal. There may be a wealth of ritual and form. There may be clearly defined and fervently defended doctrine. But unless Christ's love—received and given—fills that zeal and doctrine, there is only spiritual death, and the church fades away. Its lampstand is removed and all becomes darkness, as if Christ's light had never shined among this people. Thank God, your lampstand is still here, still ready to shine with sacred fire, the fire of God's love. Thank God there is still time!

As an angel, a holy messenger of God, I have never known the darkness of sin and death, and I never will. I have never known what it is to reign with God in heavenly glory—that is reserved for you, those who are redeemed by the blood of Christ. I am only a servant, a guardian, a caretaker. No, all these blessings in the body and blood of Christ are for you alone, human beings who are loved and chosen to be God's children even before time began.

Remember who has loved you. Return to Him. Do not let your lamp grow dim and be taken away. "He who has an ear, let him hear what the Spirit says to the churches. To him who overcomes, I will give the right to eat from the tree of life, which is in the paradise of God" (Revelation 2:7). Life, the greatest most precious gift, life that never perishes—this is God's gift to all who receive His love in Jesus.

The tree of life is not God's gift to angels. It is for people like you, people who remember and return to Jesus, their first love, something I am confident you will do. After all, why would anyone turn down the love of Jesus? By the way, though I can't eat from the tree of life, would you mind if I rejoice while you partake? It is the least you could do, considering how busy I have been keeping you out of trouble.

PRAYER

Gracious God, thank You for saving me, a sinful human being. Thank You for the love of Jesus, who died to save me. Help me remember His great love for me so He might be all in all. And Lord, thank You for my unseen friends, Your holy angels. In Jesus' name. Amen.

ASH WEDNESDAY

CHILDREN'S SERMON

Revelation 2:1–7

VISUAL AID

Candlestick with candle

THEME VERSE

These are the words of Him who holds the seven stars in His right hand
and walks among the seven golden lampstands. (Revelation 2:1)

It is good to see you here at our Ash Wednesday service. What do you
think Ash Wednesday is? *(Allow children to respond.)* Ash Wednesday is
the first day of Lent, the time before Easter. Many Christians have ashes
placed on their foreheads today to show they are sorry for their sins and
that they trust Jesus for forgiveness.

During Lent, our church has special services. This year we are thinking
about the seven churches in the Book of Revelation. We will look at what
was good about these churches and what was bad. Most important, we will
find out how each church needed Jesus to help it. The apostle John says
each church is like a lamp on a lampstand. Tonight I have brought a candle
and candlestick. The candle stands for our church.

What does the candle do? *(Allow children to respond.)* That is right, it
gives light so we can see in the dark. Could you see in this big room if there
were seven candles? *(Allow children to respond.)* Probably. What if there
was only one candle? *(Allow children to respond.)* We would be able to see,
but it would be more difficult. If we didn't have electric lights, we would
need candles so we would not hurt ourselves stumbling around in the dark.

If our church is like a candle shining in a dark world, it would be important that its light not go out. If it did go out, people might lose their way.
The light our church shines with is the Good News of God's love in Jesus.

When we tell others that Jesus died for their sins so they can be forgiven, the darkness in their lives is chased away. Peace and joy replace fear and guilt.

If we were to forget about God's love in Jesus and not tell others about it, it would be like the candle of our church going out. The candle of the church at Ephesus was in danger of going out because the people were forgetting how important the love of Jesus was. They also were forgetting to tell others about Jesus' love. So in his letter, John reminded the Christians in Ephesus of Jesus' love and the call to be Jesus' witnesses.

Let's pray that God will keep us in His love so the candle of our church will continue shining for Jesus.

PRAYER

Dear Lord Jesus, You know I love You, but sometimes my sins keep me from shining. Forgive me and help me to tell others that You have died for my sins and their sins so all of us can be forgiven, walk in Your light, and live with You forever. In Your name. Amen.

LENT 1

THE LETTER TO SMYRNA: FEAR UNTO DEATH VS. COURAGE UNTO LIFE

Isaiah 14:12–17; Revelation 2:8–11; Matthew 24:5–15

THEME VERSE:

Do not be afraid of what you are about to suffer. (Revelation 2:10a)

I realize this is somewhat awkward, to have someone you have never met bring you a special message from God. But before you blame your pastor, it is not his fault. Pastor Polycarp was reluctant to give his pulpit to someone he had never met, especially someone who literally appeared out of nowhere.

Pastor Polycarp was preparing his sermon when, in the blink of an eye, I was there. Now I had always been there, but your pastor didn't know it. Seeing me, he thought I was a stranger who was in need of his advice or a gift of love from the church. But it was only me, the angel of the parish. Pastor Polycarp was slow to accept the idea that I was an angel, but the building was securely locked and still I was standing there. He concluded that I must be who I said I was, and I am an angel.

But I am not just any angel. I am your angel, the angel assigned to the church at Smyrna. I have been sent to you from the Lord Jesus Christ by way of your beloved apostle John, friend and teacher of your pastor, Polycarp. John wants me to tell you that he prays for you every day. Indeed, he is far more concerned for your well-being than he is for his own, though he is a prisoner on Patmos and you are free, at least for a while. You see, what has happened to John and to the other apostles—namely, martyrdom and prison—lies ahead for many of you.

You may call me Stephanos, "the crowned one." There are good reasons for me to take that name. Your great city of Smyrna is known as a crown. Rome calls you "the lovely, the crown of Ionia, the ornament of Asia." Yet those attributes that inspire this name are of little value. The reference brings to mind the religious character of the people here, people of devotion, but not to the God who made heaven and earth. No, the people are devoted to the state, which to the residents of Smyrna has become its god. Smyrna was the first city in the Roman Empire to build a temple to the goddess Rome. Along with her temple are ones dedicated to Tiberius, son of Augustus, and to Livia. There is even a temple to the Roman Senate. It is as if your neighbors will do anything to curry favor with the current masters of the world. In exchange for this debasement, your fair city receives a library, a theater, a stadium. These edifices are beautiful now, but in a few years, they will be piles of broken stone, just as Rome will be.

But you and your neighbors have little in common. Your faith has kept you from running with the idolaters. You have stood fast and refused to worship those pitiful idols Rome calls its gods. Because of this, you already are suffering: an occasional arrest, a key leader flogged and imprisoned. Soon you will suffer more. Some of the Jews who claim to be God's children have allied themselves with the pagans who oppose you. These enemies claim that you are traitors to Rome. Although pagan and Jew are hostile to each other, they hate Christ even more. Therefore, they hate you, Christ's followers.

Besides all this, you live amid poverty, barely able to feed, clothe, and house your families. Your neighbors don't want to hire atheists and cannibals, which is what they consider you to be. Because you have cast aside the gods of Greece and Rome, gods that can be seen, your neighbors believe you have no god at all. You are atheists. Surely a people who practice human sacrifice, eating and drinking the blood of the victim, are the most unsavory sort. It is all untrue, of course. It is all a misunderstanding of your faith, but that is why your enemies hate you and want to be rid of you. No wonder you are afraid.

But don't be afraid! I bring you Jesus' own words written in John's hand. These are words of encouragement. I bring you a message from "the First and the Last, who died and came to life again" (Revelation 2:8). Because He who was crucified now lives, every problem you face is temporary, a moment not worth comparing to the glory prepared for you. Rome, your pagan enemies, the lying fanatics, they all will be gone in no time. But not Jesus. Jesus is the one who existed before all else, who died, and who now lives to defend you. Soon you will enjoy the fullness of His victory. No matter how terrible the events ahead, you are on the winning side, Jesus' side. Nothing can harm you because nothing can harm your resurrected Savior.

Perhaps you wonder if Jesus even notices what you endure each day in your service to Him. He most certainly does. "I know your afflictions and your poverty," He says reassuringly, "yet you are rich!" (Revelation 2:9). And you are! Does pagan Smyrna have what you have? You possess the treasures of God's Law and Gospel, His grace, the forgiveness of sins, citizenship in God's eternal kingdom, membership in the family of believers in Christ, a family that cares deeply for you. Smyrna thinks of itself as a glorious crown, but it is all tin and rhinestones compared to what God has given you in Christ.

What of those accusations from unbelieving Jews who have allied themselves with the idol worshipers against you? Don't you think Jesus is aware of that too? He says, "I know the slander of those who say they are Jews and are not, but are a synagogue of Satan" (Revelation 2:9). These Jews say you are traitors to Rome. But how could that be when you pray daily for your emperor and governor? Your only crime, if it is a crime, is that you don't worship your rulers. Those who claim Moses as their lawgiver should remember his command not to bear false witness. May they, who first had the Law, repent of their slander before it is too late. It is not you but these false Jews who have reason to be afraid.

So, friends of Christ at Smyrna and Pastor Polycarp, don't be afraid. Yes, you will suffer—some of you a great deal, especially you, Polycarp. You, dear pastor, will continue to serve in this place for many years, defending the faith not only against pagans and unbelieving Jews but also against Christian heretics and Gnostics. There are troubles ahead that you can't even imagine.

False teachers, dangerous wolves as yet unseen in Smyrna, will undermine the apostolic faith. Marcion will deny that the God who created the world is the Father of the Lord Jesus Christ. He will claim there is nothing to God but love, that an evil, false god was responsible for the suffering and death of Jesus. Then Valentinus will convince many that everything physical is evil, that the spiritual world alone is good, that heaven is made up of pairs of "aeons"—angel-like, almost divine beings, one of which fell into sin and created the world. To Valentinus, even Christ is an aeon that adopted a human body.

Many will consider this nonsense to be wisdom, but Polycarp will know better. He will defend the truth of the Trinity, the truth of the divine and human natures of Christ, the truth of Jesus' death, burial, and resurrection for sinners. Polycarp will be a giant of faith and orthodoxy, doing battle with every enemy of Jesus. He will be arrested at a public festival and given the opportunity to renounce his faith. He will refuse, proclaiming that he has served Christ for 86 years and is not about to deny him now. Then Pastor Polycarp will be burned to death, as may some of you.

But don't be afraid, Jesus says. It is a trial you must go through, but His grace is sufficient for what lies ahead. Persecution will last only ten days. Will it last literally ten twenty-four-hour days? No, that is not what John and the Spirit of Jesus are telling you. Ten days means there is a limit. When the testing is complete, the suffering will end. For some of you, that will be the day you die in faith, as it will be for Polycarp. For others, it will be when persecution ends and you can live out your years peacefully. But the persecution will end. That is a promise from Jesus.

Therefore, Jesus exhorts you to "be faithful, even to the point of death, and I will give you the crown of life" (Revelation 2:10). Many of you seem so troubled by death, so anxious that you will do anything to forestall it. Why? For an unbeliever, death is understandably a terrible thing. It is blackness. It is a nightmare of the unknown. It is a den of horrors. But not for you. For you, death is a door to something far better—a place of light and peace in the presence of Jesus, whom you will at last see face-to-face.

Have you not repeatedly recited the words of the precious psalm: "Even though I walk through the valley of the shadow of death, I will fear no evil, for You are with me" (Psalm 23:4). How can you fear the valley if your Savior has trod its path ahead of you and returns to carry you safely through it? Fear is what happens when your gaze dwells on your circumstances rather than on Jesus' face. Lift up your heads from all these things that frighten you and rest your gaze on the King of glory! As you do, you will find your heart encouraged to keep going, to stay in the race and finish it. Then you will receive the promised crown of life. This is not a crown worn by kings, one heavy with gold and jewels. It is not a crown that someone wears whether or not he or she deserves it. That is not the crown to which you look forward. Yours is a crown of living laurel, woven into a ring, a crown like that worn by the athlete who labored for it, who sweated and struggled and agonized, every muscle straining to finish the race.

And you will finish because Jesus has run the race for you and won. He is there at the end of the course, calling you. The Holy Spirit dwells within you, making you a holy temple for Christ. God's angels like me are caring for you, lifting you up when you stumble. Thus the crown, a crown of life eternal, is yours as you receive it by means of faith, as Word and Sacrament keep it before your eyes. If this is the prize of your heart, the prize for which you yearn, every resource of God's grace will empower you to receive it.

Do you hear me, Smyrna? Do you hear me, all who will read this letter in the years to come? Suffering lies ahead. You may not suffer like Polycarp, burned to death as the mob laughed and cheered, but you will suffer. Perhaps your suffering will be from the pain of faithless friends. Maybe your suffering will result from the rejection of those who spurn your faith. Maybe you will feel alone in your service of God because your loved ones feel no need for Jesus. Your Savior understands your suffering. One day you will see for yourself that it wasn't in vain. Keep the eyes of your faith on the crown Jesus promises, knowing that "He who overcomes will not be hurt at all by the second death" (Revelation 2:11).

Remember, you are never alone. Your angel may be sitting right beside you now. I have stood beside Pastor Polycarp many times as he wrote his sermons, though he never knew it until today. From the way he is looking at me, I can tell that he would like his pulpit back. So with your permission, I will return to my guardpost on your behalf.

PRAYER

Dear Jesus, thank You for the privilege of serving You even when that means suffering. Help me always to know that a crown of life, paid for by Your precious blood, is mine, waiting for me at the end of my course. Give me courage and faith to persevere. In Your name I pray. Amen.

LENT 1

CHILDREN'S SERMON

Revelation 2:8–11

VISUAL AIDS

Bicycle helmet   Large stick

THEME VERSE

Do not be afraid of what you are about to suffer. (Revelation 2:10a)

Hi, kids. It is good to see so many of you again. In the lesson from Revelation for today, God's Word tells us not to be afraid of suffering. That is easy to say but hard to do. What are some things of which you are afraid? *(Allow children to respond.)* Some people are afraid of snakes. Some people are afraid of the dark. Sometimes it is okay to be afraid because fear can keep us away from things that can hurt us.

I have brought a big stick with me. Would someone like to be hit on the head with it? *(Look around as if surprised.)* What? There is no one who wants to be hit on the head? Why not? *(Allow children to respond.)* Oh, because it would hurt. It would be foolish to let someone hit you on the head with a big stick.

Look at what else I brought. It is a helmet. Who would like to wear it? *(Choose a volunteer and put the helmet on the child.)* Why do we wear helmets like this one? *(Allow children to respond.)* Yes, we wear a helmet to protect ourselves from getting hurt, especially when we ride a bicycle or scooter or skateboard. We may fall down, but we have protection from being badly injured.

Christians have a helmet that keeps us from all spiritual harm. Our helmet is the Lord Jesus Christ. He died for all our sins and rose again so the devil cannot harm us. Even if we suffer, we are protected. When we die, we have a home in heaven with Jesus and His promise of a wonderful new body like His when He comes back someday.

Therefore, we don't need to be afraid when people make fun of us for loving Jesus. We don't need to be afraid when people threaten us or try to make us do wrong things. Jesus will keep us safe forever. He knows what is happening to us every minute. He is with us all the time. We are never helpless nor alone. Our Baptism is God's promise that all this is true. Let's thank Jesus for protecting us.

PRAYER

Dear Jesus, often I feel alone and afraid. Sometimes people make fun of me or threaten to hurt me, but I know I am not alone. Jesus, You are with me, and You promise to keep me safe in Your love. Help me to be brave and always to trust You. In Your strong name I pray. Amen.

LENT 2

THE LETTER TO PERGAMUM: IDOLATRY IS THE DEADLIEST SIN

Numbers 22:1–20; Revelation 2:12–17; John 6:26–33

THEME VERSE

You have people there who hold to the teaching of Balaam.
(Revelation 2:14a)

I know what you are wondering. What is a strange man dressed in a white robe and carrying a double-edged sword doing in this peace-loving church? Why is he in this pulpit? Might he be here to slay you as they did Brother Antipas, a man whose courage and faith continue to inspire so many?

No. I am not an agent of Caesar on a mission of death. I am an agent of the King, the Lord Jesus, who has sent me on a mission of life. I am your angel, the angel of this church. Distomos, "Two-Edged," is my name. Let me remind you of the double-edged sword of Jesus, a sword that comforts and defends His people yet also judges and slays the unrepentant who cling to idols. I have come to you from John, the apostle of love, who is held prisoner on Patmos, a lonely island two hundred miles south of here. He sends you greetings and assurances of his prayers amid your trials, living as you do in this pagan and immoral city.

To your neighbors, religious pluralism is one of the highest virtues. They see no reason for an exclusive faith. In fact, because you refuse to acknowledge any god but the Holy Trinity and because you reject the countless other deities worshiped in your community, your neighbors see you as a threat. You are considered intolerant, undesirable. You are labeled enemies of the state.

What an insult you are to religious Pergamum—wealthy, educated, and sophisticated Pergamum. Your city once had a library of 200,000 volumes before the books were carted off to Egypt by Marc Antony. Parchment, the finest and most long-lasting writing surface, was invented here. On the hill against which Pergamum is built are hundreds of temples dedicated to every god imaginable. A colossal altar to Zeus, chief of all the Greek gods, is carved from the mountain's solid rock. There are temples to Athena, Dionysus, and even Asclepius, the god of medicine. Of course, no truly Roman city would be complete without temples to the divine Augustus and the goddess Rome, focuses of the imperial cult. There is even a monument to "the unknown god," should one perhaps have been left out.

As religious as your neighbors clearly are, they find it deeply offensive that you do not join them in their festivals or invite them to yours. They consider your doctrine that only baptized believers in Christ have a home in His kingdom and a place at His table to be rude. They consider you to be judgmental and intolerant because you do not participate in the immoral rites of the numerous pagan temples. You do not associate with them, which makes your neighbors angry.

But your neighbors are more than angry. They are enraged to the point of murder as they oppose all for which you stand. That is why John sent me to you to speak these words of Jesus: "I know where you live—where Satan has his throne" (Revelation 2:13). With every god but Christ exalted in Pergamum, it is no wonder that your suffering has intensified, as it has for your brethren in sister congregations. Many of you watched helplessly as Brother Antipas was put to death because he refused to recognize all the gods as being equally divine with Jesus. Although his martyrdom terrified you beyond words, you remain faithful.

But you have a more subtle enemy, one not from outside the congregation at Pergamum but from within the church. Some claim you can be faithful to Christ while adopting the values and way of life practiced by the pagans. Such individuals are among you, and so far you have tolerated them. "I have a few things against you," says the Lord Jesus, "you have people there who hold to the teaching of Balaam, who taught Balak to entice the Israelites to sin by eating food sacrificed to idols and by committing sexual immorality" (Revelation 2:14).

You remember the story of Balaam, don't you? He was hired by Balak, the king of Moab, to curse the Israelites who were on their way from the desert to the Promised Land. No one had been able to stop them. The Amorites had fallen before them, and Moab was next in line. "I will reward you handsomely and do whatever you say. Come and put a curse on these people for me," King Balak had pleaded with Balaam, a renowned pagan prophet. (See Numbers 22ff.)

But no matter how hard he tried, Balaam could not curse the Israelites. All he could utter was blessing upon blessing for Israel, so he tried another tactic. Balaam would get the Israelites to make spiritual and moral compromises. If he could coax the Israelite men into the tents of the Moabite women, Israel's threat would be neutralized. It almost worked. The Bible says, "The [Israelite] men began to indulge in sexual immorality with Moabite women, who invited them to the sacrifices to their gods" (Numbers 25:1–2). The result was a plague on Israel that didn't end until the leaders of this apostasy were put to death.

Balaam has been dead for centuries, but his spirit lives on in people such as the Nicolaitans. These followers of Nicolas advocate spiritual and moral compromise in the church at Pergamum and in many other congregations. Believe in Jesus, Nicolas says, but join the party too. What could be wrong with a meal at the temple of Zeus or Athena if it promotes civic unity? Why not join in the fun with the temple prostitutes? In fact, why not do whatever you please? After all, our God is a God of grace. He forgives us in advance.

Good Christians of Pergamum, turn a deaf ear to these poisonous words. They are nothing more than the lies of Satan. Have you not heard the words of St. Paul, who, like Antipas, died for the faith? "What shall we say, then?" asks Paul. "Shall we go on sinning so that grace may increase? By no means! We died to sin; how can we live in it any longer? Or don't you know that all of us who were baptized into Christ Jesus were baptized into His death? We were therefore buried with Him through baptism into death in order that, just as Christ was raised from the dead through the glory of the Father, we too may live a new life" (Romans 6:1–4).

Dying to sin and living to righteousness—this is the calling of those baptized into Jesus. Enabled by the Holy Spirit through the Word of Christ. They say no to Balaam and his lies. They say no to the easy, compromising religion of Nicolas. They say yes to the faith of Antipas, who followed Jesus even to the point of death.

Ultimately, this double-edged sword of Jesus is no threat to the faithful Christian, though Christians, like all people, need to repent. The sword has two edges for a reason. One edge is for judgment. It proclaims the wrath of God to all who will not repent of sin and seek His mercy. This is the edge reserved for Balaam and Nicolas and their followers, for those who choose idolatry and immorality and spurn God's offer of grace and forgiveness in Jesus. It is the sharpened edge of God's Law that, when violated, earns His retribution. The other edge of the sword of Christ defends the humble sinner who comes to God for mercy. This edge slays every enemy of the soul: sin, death, and the devil. This edge eternally protects all who hide behind it. It is the comforting edge of the Gospel, which never cuts but always heals and saves. May you find yourself behind the Gospel edge. "Repent therefore!" Jesus pleads with you. "Otherwise, I will soon come to you and will fight against them with the sword of My mouth" (Revelation 2:16). There's one sword and two edges: One to fight for you, and one to fight against you. Which will it be?

Jesus and His servant John have confidence that you will choose the Gospel edge. Why? Because you are standing firm in faith. "Yet you remain true to My name," says your Lord. "You did not renounce your faith in Me, even in the days of Antipas, My faithful witness, who was put to death in your city" (Revelation 2:13). Well done! Continue to stand firm! As you do, there's a promise to you from the Holy Spirit: "To him who overcomes, I will give some of the hidden manna" (Revelation 2:17). This manna is God's gift to all for whom Jesus has died and who have been baptized in Him. In the desert, God's people were fed and sustained by a food that miraculously appeared each day. For all the years of their wanderings, manna was always available. But once in the Promised Land, a land flowing with milk and honey, manna was no longer needed, and it disappeared.

So it is for you who live in a hostile city surrounded by the enemies of Jesus. Heavenly food graces your table each time you celebrate the Lord's Supper. Jesus is present, miraculously strengthening you, sustaining you, and defending you. But one day the Holy Meal of His body and blood will no longer be necessary because you will see your Lord face-to-face and join Him at the eternal feast in heaven.

How can you be sure of this future reality? Because of the white stone of innocence. "To him who overcomes," says Jesus, "I will also give . . . a white stone with a new name written on it" (Revelation 2:17). All the acquitted, all those who are declared not guilty, possess this white stone. The divine Judge has heard the charges against you. He has seen the wounded body of Jesus, His arms outstretched, pleading for you. He has seen the garments of Christ's righteousness covering you in Baptism. The decision has been reached. Almighty God has taken out the two stones—the black one for guilt and the white one for innocence. By His grace in Christ Jesus, the white stone of acquittal has been given to you. On it is inscribed your new name, a name that declares you to be a child of God, a forgiven sinner, one who is righteous by faith.

This completes my assignment for today. Although my name means "two-edged" and my words have been sharp, remember that I am the angel of your church. You may not see me, but you can be sure I will be here.

Prayer

Lord, like many of Your people before me, I live in a place and time in which evil and idolatry threaten to overwhelm true faith and righteousness. Give me courage to remain faithful no matter the temptation. Help me discern right from wrong that I might not be deceived. Thank You that in Baptism You have declared me to be God's child forever. In Jesus' name. Amen.

LENT 2

CHILDREN'S SERMON

Revelation 2:17

VISUAL AID

Plastic or wooden toy broadsword

THEME VERSE

These are the words of Him who has the sharp, double-edged sword.
(Revelation 2:12b)

Hello, children, and welcome. It looks real, but it is only a toy. What do you think of this sword? *(Invite several children to hold and/or touch the sword.)* What are swords used for? *(Allow children to respond.)* Yes, swords were used to fight. Today soldiers don't use swords to fight. They are used only as decoration or for ceremonies. But hundreds of years ago, most soldiers would have carried swords when they went into battle.

How many edges does this sword have? *(Allow children to respond.)* Yes, my sword has two edges. If it were real, a soldier could hold it with two hands and swing it from side to side and it would cut either way. *(Demonstrate.)* Soldiers could attack an enemy with a sword or defend someone with a sword

The Bible uses the sword as a symbol for God's Word. In Ephesians, Paul speaks of the "sword of the Spirit, which is the word of God" (Ephesians 6:17). In Revelation, John speaks of the sword of Jesus' mouth. Just as a metal sword can attack or defend, so can the sword of Jesus' word.

You and I are God's children. Jesus loves us and died for us. Jesus promises in His Word to keep us safe from every enemy, especially sin and the devil. When we trust Jesus, it is as if He is out in front of us, fighting off every attacker who would hurt us. For us, Jesus' sword is not something to be afraid of but something to hide behind because it protects us.

For people who don't love God and who don't care if they sin or not, the sword of Jesus' word can be frightening because it strikes back and forth in their hearts to show them they have chosen a dangerous path. If they keep going along that path, someday they will be lost forever. But if the sword of Jesus' word turns them back to God, then they will find that His sword defends them and takes care of them.

I pray that all of us are on the right path, the path of faith in Jesus. On that path, we are always safe and the sword of God's Word protects us. Let's pray that we will hide behind Jesus' sword and that many others will want to join us there.

Prayer

Dear Jesus, thank You for the sword of Your Word that turns me from the wrong path when I am tempted to fall away from You. Thank You also for protecting me from every danger as I trust in You. Help others to hear Your Word and come to faith in You. In Your holy name I pray. Amen.

LENT 3

THE LETTER TO THYATIRA: IMMORALITY, HIGHWAY TO THE GRAVE

1 Kings 16:29–33; Revelation 2:18–29; Matthew 25:31–46

THEME VERSE

You tolerate that woman Jezebel . . . . I have given her time to repent of
her immorality, but she is unwilling. (Revelation 2:20–21)

This is one hardworking congregation, not only in church work but also in the market, factory, and workshop! After serving you all these years, I must admit that I am impressed. The purple fabric you make and sell is as fine as any that can be found in the Roman Empire. You are solid citizens. You even take time away from work to attend church, though it costs you money. What character!

I know all this because I am Aster. I have been your angel for the past thirty years or so. Aster means "star," so my name reminds you of my master, the Lord Jesus Christ, the Morning Star. His coming, past and future, signals a bright new day with light that chases away the darkness of ignorance, fear, and guilt. Jesus is the light of the world. His Word brings true enlightenment, the knowledge of salvation. When He died on the cross for the sins of the world, darkness covered the earth. Yet at that moment, the light of salvation dawned on the whole human race. I am not the light, I reflect His light while I serve as your guardian and bring you God's message. Jesus is the true light.

Jesus has assigned me to your congregation. Although you don't see much of me, this is my church too. And being your angel is becoming more difficult as the church continues to grow. Instead of leaving the sinful ways of the world behind, some Christians bring the world into the church. That troubles Jesus, as it does the apostle John, who suffers as a prisoner for the faith on the island of Patmos. Together they've given me a special letter to share with you. This message is not a suggestion for improvement. It is a life-and-death message from the divine Son of God "whose eyes are like blazing fire and whose feet are like burnished bronze" (Revelation 2:18). My superior and yours, the King of kings and Lord of lords, wants you to know that He is the one to whom all humanity will give account. And He *will* be heard.

But don't be afraid! Be assured that though He is Lord of heaven and earth, Jesus loves you, and through faith, He is pleased with you. All your sins are washed away. You are makers of purple cloth, but in Holy Baptism, all of you are clothed in the white robes of righteousness. God is pleased with you today. He has accepted you because of the sacrifice of His Son, Jesus Christ. Your congregation is known throughout Asia for your good deeds, your love of God and neighbor, your firm adherence to the faith of the apostles. Indeed, "you are now doing more than you did at first" (Revelation 2:19). This may be true, but it is more difficult than ever to be a Christian in Thyatira.

The threat to godliness you face is different than the challenges placed before your fellow believers in Smyrna, Ephesus, and other cities. They are assaulted daily by the emperor cult, the extravagances of wealth, the arrogance of those steeped in philosophy. But Thyatira is a small town of working people—craftspeople and merchants. There are no temples to Rome or Caesar to contend with in Thyatira, only the usual shrines to Artemis and Apollo. High culture and religious zeal have not put Thyatira on the map; rather, it is the water in your rivers, which is perfect for dying cloth, and the quality of your products, which are sought-after by the rich. Although lacking in cultural amenities, Thyatira has its share of temptations. The devil hasn't left you alone because yours is a small town. Perhaps it is even harder to be a faithful Christian here. Being small means each of you knows everyone else's business intimately, intensifying the pressure to conform.

This raises the matter of your craft guilds. If you make and sell a product, such as the lovely purple cloth for which Thyatira is famous, you are expected to be a member of the guild. If you don't join, your business suffers. People will not buy cloth from you. Neighbors will not talk to you. To survive economically, it is almost essential to join a guild. But as you have discovered, joining a guild can place a Christian in some awkward situations. Membership in a craft guild is more than showing up at the meetings and discussing quality control, new technologies, and better marketing strategies. Part of the meeting involves a meal in which everyone eats meat sacrificed to Apollo or Artemis. And several times a year, guild members participate in pagan festivals—festivals that can involve ritual sex. When you said yes to Christ, you also said no to such shameful things. But joining the guild is the key to prosperity. Stay out and your business might die.

Maybe some of you remember Lydia, a former member of your community, a Gentile like yourselves but also a God-fearing woman. She would not "pay her dues," so to speak. As a dealer in purple fabric like many of you, she chose to move to Philippi to remain in business. Since you last saw her, she has become a baptized Christian. Upon hearing Paul preach the Good News of Jesus' suffering and death for her sins and His resurrection from the dead, God opened Lydia's heart to believe. She became so dedicated to Christ that the first meeting place of the church at Philippi was in her home. God has richly blessed faithful Lydia. Consider her example of faithfulness and imitate it.

Some of you continue to struggle with your decision. It would be so easy to compromise and join the craft guild. "Those gods they worship aren't really gods," you might reason, "so what difference does it make if I eat a little sacrificial meat?" That is what Jezebel is trying to tell you, that compromising woman you have in the congregation. "Jezebel" is not her real name, of course, but you know the person of whom I am speaking. The original Jezebel, the namesake of the woman in your congregation, was Ahab's wife. She was the Baal-worshiping daughter of the king of Tyre and Sidon. Her goal in life was to destroy Israel's faith in Yahweh. Jezebel invited the prophets of Baal to eat at the king's table. Jezebel slaughtered hundreds of Yahweh's prophets. Jezebel brought false charges against Naboth so he would be killed and she could seize his vineyard as a gift for her husband.

Because of Jezebel's evil influence, all the members of the royal family died violent deaths—her husband, Ahab; her sons; and all who might have a claim to Israel's throne. When they were all dead, Jezebel tried to seduce the new king of Israel, Jehu. With painted eyes and a fancy hairdo, she appeared in a tower window of the palace, welcoming Jehu to her bed. He wasn't impressed. Instead, Jehu called to her servants, "If you are on my side, throw her down." They did. Her body was left unburied and was eaten by dogs. (See 2 Kings 9:30–37.)

All the ugliness of Jezebel's story could become the story of this church at Thyatira if you listen to this woman, if you begin compromising, if you believe you can serve Jesus and the false gods of your neighbors as well, if you believe you can enjoy the forgiveness of sins and continue to indulge in a promiscuous lifestyle. Make no mistake, you can't.

Some of you might think your behavior and beliefs are a private matter. You might think no one else will notice or be affected. But Holy Scripture says: "None of us lives to himself alone and none of us dies to himself alone" (Romans 14:7). All you do and say is observed and evaluated by others and has an impact on their lives. Ahab's entire family died because of the evil he allowed into his home through Jezebel. And Jesus says to you, "I will make those who commit adultery with her suffer intensely, unless they repent of her ways. . . . I will strike her children dead" (Revelation 2:22–23).

Jesus does not mean physical death, He means spiritual death. He means a journey to the grim doors of hell because the heart is calloused by false doctrine and immoral behavior. This journey involves a growing darkness of mind and heart, and infection with fear and guilt, which eat away at the soul. Before you come to hell, it comes to you. Worse, if you continue on this spiritual journey, others—friends and family who love and trust you—will imitate what you do and bring on themselves the same fate. Although you think your actions are done in secret, they never are. The one who has "eyes like blazing fire" always knows (Revelation 2:18). "I am He who searches hearts and minds," says the Son of God who is coming in judgment. "I will repay each of you according to your deeds" (Revelation 2:23).

To this point, your deeds have been the deeds of faith, love, service, and perseverance as my master, Jesus, said at the beginning of my message to you. These deeds of love have been given to you by the Holy Spirit, who strengthens your faith through God's Word and the Sacraments. Through these means of grace, God keeps you steadfast in the one true faith. Continue in this faith and dedication. "Hold on to what you have until I come," says your Lord (Revelation 2:23). He will help you. Your suffering will last only a little while. Remember this when you feel the temptation to compromise. You have needs, but Jesus knows all about them and still cares for you. He promised you in the Sermon on the Mount: "Seek first [God's] kingdom and His righteousness and all these things [all that you need] will be given to you as well" (Matthew 6:33).

People of Thyatira, you have entrusted Jesus with your eternal soul, your ultimate destiny. You have believed that He died for you and lives again, forgiving all your sins and earning for you a place in heaven. If you trust Jesus for all this, can't you trust Him to meet your daily needs? The apostle Paul has written: "He who did not spare His own Son, but gave Him up for us all—how will He not also, along with Him, graciously give us all things?" (Romans 8:32).

It may look as if your needs will not be met without compromising your faith and values, but that is Jezebel's lie. Look where listening to her got Ahab and his family. Jesus wants nothing but good for you, and as you remain in Him by faith, you will experience His goodness in abundance. He says: "To him who overcomes and does My will to the end, I will give authority over the nations" (Revelation 2:26). Why submit to the compromising authority of some Jezebel or any other influence that would rob you of a peaceful conscience and enslave you? You have the promise of Jesus that you will reign with Him in heaven. Why "give in" when you can "go up" and spend eternity with Jesus, the bright morning star?

Well, if I stay here much longer, you might start thinking of me as the "star" attraction. But I am your angel, Aster. Only Jesus, the Morning Star, will take you safely past all the threatening Jezebels to the Promised Land where He is king and royal purple isn't what you sell but what you wear.

PRAYER

O Lord Jesus, Star of the Morning, make me deaf to the attractions of this world and let me hear only Your calling to a holy life of faith. May I remain close to the cross where Your death bought me from sin and made me Your child. May I always find refuge in the empty tomb where Satan was defeated and Your victory was made mine forever. In Your holy name I pray. Amen.

LENT 3

CHILDREN'S SERMON

Revelation 2:18–29

VISUAL AIDS

Box or sheet of self-stick gold stars

THEME VERSE

To him who overcomes . . . I will also give . . . the morning star.
(Revelation 2:26, 28)

Hi, boys and girls! I am so glad you are here. Do you like gold stars? *(Allow children to respond.)* I remember when I was in elementary school, sometimes the teacher would put a gold star on my paper when I did something good or received a good grade on an assignment. Have you ever received a gold star? *(Allow children to respond.)* Why did you get a gold star? *(Allow children to respond.)*

In the Bible lesson for today, John describes Jesus as the "morning star." Have you ever seen a star so bright that it continues to shine even after the sun rises? The planet Venus is sometimes that bright. Just as the bright morning star tells us a brand-new day has begun, so Jesus shines in our lives, telling us that everything is fresh and new by faith in Him. When we trust Jesus as our Savior, we know our sins are forgiven and we get to start over every day.

I would like to give each of you a gold star to remind you that Jesus is shining on you with His love and forgiveness and showing you the way to a happy life. *(Pass out the stars.)* The star I am giving you also reminds you that when we get to heaven we will see Jesus for ourselves. Right now we hear about Jesus and believe He is with us, but we don't see Him, do we? *(Allow children to respond.)* In heaven we will see Jesus. We won't need stickers to remind us of who Jesus is and what He has done for us because we will be with Him forever. Seeing Jesus, our morning star, will be our greatest joy when we get to heaven.

Let's praise God for Jesus, our bright morning star.

PRAYER

Thank You, Jesus, that You are the morning star that shines in my life. As I trust Your Word, Your light shows me the way to happiness. Because You love me and died for me, I know my sins are forgiven and I have a home in heaven where You will be my star forever. In Your name I pray. Amen.

LENT 4

THE LETTER TO SARDIS: LETHARGY—SLOW DEATH

Isaiah 29:13–16; Revelation 3:1–6; Matthew 24:42–51

THEME VERSE

Wake up! Strengthen what remains and is about to die for I have not found your deeds complete in the sight of My God. (Revelation 3:2)

This is not my favorite task, scolding you. I would just as soon put it off indefinitely. But our Lord Jesus Christ, whom I serve, has given me a job, and I am going to do it. But first let me introduce myself. I am Gregory, your angel. My name means "watchful," which is what Jesus wants you, the Christians at Sardis, to do: Remain alert with a watchfulness that translates into devotion and good deeds—things you have been lacking.

Why am I, an angel, telling you these things? Because that is what we angels do. Our job is to serve God by looking out for you, defending you when necessary, and bringing you messages from your Savior and King. You have not seen me till now because I prefer to remain invisible. But I have been with you for years. I have just come from meeting with the Lord and with the apostle John. The words I have for you were written by John but spoken by Jesus Himself. So wake up and take notice!

To be blunt, that is why I am standing before you today. I am here to give you a wake-up call. You seem to have become complacent, lazy, lethargic. Your faith could be likened to the history of your city: Sardis, once glorious and wealthy, is now a poor backwater town, neglected by those in power. You continue to make beautiful cloth and jewelry, but things in Sardis are in a state of cultural and economic decline. Croesus, the richest king in the world, whose palace once graced your city, would hardly recognize Sardis now.

Nor would the apostles—all of whom but John have been martyred for Christ—recognize your faith. They died rather than compromise the truth of the Gospel. But you have chosen an easy faith and an easy morality, fitting in with the pagans around you, becoming barely identifiable as Christians. Perhaps this is the result of the worship of Cybele, whose cult is so strong in Sardis. Her temple may have been destroyed and the temple of Artemis built in its place, but to your neighbors, Cybele and Artemis are one and the same.

I wonder if your careless regard for Christ is because you see little difference between Him and the gods of your neighbors. You see a resemblance between Cybele, the mother goddess, and Mary, the mother of Jesus. As Cybele is considered to be the mother of the god Attis, you think of Mary as the mother of the God-man, Jesus. Therefore, Mary is a goddess to be worshiped. As Attis is supposed to have killed himself and been resurrected, you think Jesus is just another resurrected god. Cybele and Attis have sacrificial meals in their honor; so does Jesus. The resurrection of Attis is celebrated in the spring; so is that of Jesus. It is all the same, you think. One person follows this god, another that god, but each path has the same goal: eternal life with the god of one's choosing. If this is how you think, no wonder you have lost your zeal for Christ. No wonder you care so little if your neighbor has heard of Jesus, of His life and death for sinners. No wonder you have no sense of urgency, no fire in your hearts for a holy life and the conversion of your friends and relatives.

Did it ever occur to you that the superficial resemblance between the cult of Cybele and the faith of Christ are intentional deceptions of the devil? Why is it that just when the Good News of salvation in Jesus is being proclaimed everywhere, all these mystery religions appear, claiming to offer the same benefits? A few years from now, the Christian theologian Tertullian will say that Satan is the author of these deceptions, and he will be right.

"Wake up! Strengthen what remains and is about to die, for I have not found your deeds complete in the sight of My God," says your Lord. "Remember, therefore, what you have received and heard; obey it, and repent" (Revelation 3:2–3). The Lord Christ is jealous for you. In the agonies of the cross, He spent His life's blood for you. He gave His life to forgive your sins. He rose again to give you new life in Him. He will not share you with another. Jesus is yours, and you are His. Now, in Jesus, you stand before God as innocent and undefiled as He is. Of course, you are sinners, but God has declared you righteous because of Jesus, who was innocent but was declared guilty for the purpose of your redemption. All your sins are now washed away, including the ones of which I accuse you. So wake up, I say. Welcome the Holy Spirit of God that stirs the flame of faith within you, and put away these evil things. This is the will of God. If you ask for His help, He will give it to you. He will enable you to repent, to put away false doctrine, and to turn to Him in faith and love. Alive by His grace alone, you will eat at the Lord's Table, receiving His body and blood. You will not eat at the table of Cybele, the table of demons. By grace, you received in Baptism a new life of righteousness in Christ and rejected the false and immoral values of the world. Christ will not share you with another.

It is time to wake up. "If you do not wake up," says Jesus, "I will come like a thief, and you will not know at what time I will come to you" (Revelation 3:3). He came in love and mercy to redeem you, to offer Himself as the all-sufficient sacrifice for your sins. Jesus came to commute the death sentence you deserve and to bring you God's pardon. Jesus' saving work was finished at the cross and the empty tomb. Now God is kindly disposed toward you and all sinners. His welcoming arms of grace are spread wide to receive you.

But the day of grace is quickly coming to an end. One day Jesus will return. He will come as the long-awaited Savior to all who have loved Him but as the dreaded judge to all who have spurned Him. The day of Jesus' coming is known only in heaven, but it will be soon, very soon. Thank God many of you will be ready. You will receive Him in faith. "Yet you have a few people in Sardis who have not soiled their clothes. They will walk with Me, dressed in white, for they are worthy" (Revelation 3:4). By faith you will be among that blessed company that is "dressed in white" and walks with Jesus, the company of those made "worthy" by faith. To be ready is to believe in Christ and to act on the basis of that belief. All good works done by faith are acceptable to God.

If this is your desire, than by faith be assured that when Jesus comes your deeds will be found complete and acceptable. A white robe of righteousness that far surpasses anything you make and sell here in Sardis will cover your sins. Not only will your sins be covered, but your name will be written in the Book of Life, never to be blotted out. When the day of Christ's coming arrives and your name is read from the book, He will proclaim in a loud voice that all will hear, "Well done, good and faithful servant! . . . Come and share your Master's happiness!" (Matthew 25:21).

Some of you are still spiritually asleep. The purpose of my visit is to warn you, to sound the alarm, to tell you to wake up. There's still time for you to repent, to complete what is lacking, to claim what is promised, to live your calling. The white garments of your Baptism are still gleaming for you. Do not delay and thereby cast them off. Leave them on!

Holy Scripture says: "Now is the time of God's favor" (2 Corinthians 6:2). "Today, if you hear His voice, do not harden your hearts" (Hebrews 3:7). "The hour has come for you to wake up from your slumber, because our salvation is nearer now than when we first believed . . . Let us put aside the deeds of darkness and put on the armor of light" (Romans 13:11–12).

Years from now, the false gods you find so tempting will be forgotten, replaced by others that are equally false and forgettable. The things Sardis has valued so highly—its textiles and jewelry—will be rotted and buried. Your great buildings will be heaps of rubble. Even the magnificent Byzantine church you will someday erect will be nothing but a ruin to be unearthed by archaeologists. Only two things will endure: the name of the triune God and your name written in the Book of Life. All who by grace believe in Jesus and repent will find their names written there.

Yes, it is difficult to go against the world, doing and believing what is right, standing up for truth when so few stand with you. Jesus and the blood of the martyrs can attest to how difficult this is. But Jesus promises that He will help you. He will give you every gift of His sevenfold Spirit. He will enable you to join Him in heaven's victory celebration. "He who has an ear, let him hear what the Spirit says to the churches" (Revelation 3:6).

My name, Gregory, says that I am watchful. And I leave you with the words of Jesus: "Wake up! Strengthen what remains . . . Obey . . . Repent" (Revelation 3:2–3). This is exactly what I am confident you will do. The Lord did not shed His blood for you for nothing. By grace, you will heed His Word, and one day, He will acknowledge your name before His Father, the company of the saints, and all the angels.

PRAYER

Gracious Lord, my zeal has often been lacking in fruit and witness for You. I have slumbered while Your Spirit has been calling me through Your Word. Awaken my deaf ears and enable me to do the works of love and faith You desire. In Jesus' holy name I pray. Amen.

LENT 4

CHILDREN'S SERMON

Revelation 3:1–6

VISUAL AID

Wind-up alarm clock

THEME VERSE

Wake up! Strengthen what remains and is about to die, for I have not found your deeds complete in the sight of My God. (Revelation 3:2)

Welcome, children! How many of you like it when the time changes in the spring? *(Allow children to respond.)* I like it because we get an extra hour of daylight. But I also dislike it because I have to wake up an hour earlier. To make sure I get out of bed, I have an alarm clock.

What time do you have to get up? *(Allow children to respond.)* Let's set the alarm for that time. *(Set the alarm.)* Now I will pull out the button, and when that time comes, the alarm will go off, like this. *(Turn knob until alarm sounds.)* Annoying, isn't it? If it wasn't annoying, we probably would not wake up. We would stay in bed and miss school or work or our appointments. If we missed the things we were supposed to do, we would be embarrassed. So like it or not, we need alarm clocks.

In our Bible lesson, Jesus tells us it is time to wake up. Many people in the church are spiritually asleep when they should be awake and doing the things that please God. We all have heard God's Word and know what He wants us to do, but we still don't do it. Why don't we pay attention to God's Word? *(Allow children to respond.)* Yes, the reason we hear but don't obey God's Word is sin. Sometimes it is hard to do God's will. Sometimes our friends don't want us to obey God. Sometimes it is more fun to do something that is wrong. Sometimes we don't want anyone to know that we are Christians.

But Jesus tells us to remember what we have seen and heard. We are to remember that He loves us. We are to remember that He died for our sins.

We are to remember that He helps us to do His will. We are to remember that He is preparing a home for us in heaven. When we believe and remember all these things, we wake up and obey Jesus again. As we do, we grow happier and others want to learn about Jesus too. Let's pray that Jesus will help us wake up every day, eager to serve Him.

PRAYER

Dear Lord Jesus, I am sorry that I am sometimes sleeping when You are talking to me. Help me wake up every day to Your voice. Help me to learn and grow and do the things You want. Thank You for dying for me that I might have a new life today and in heaven with You forever. In Your name I pray. Amen.

LENT 5

THE LETTER TO PHILADELPHIA:
NEGLECT—LOCKED OUT IN DEATH'S NIGHT

Isaiah 60:3–11; Revelation 3:7–13; Matthew 28:16–20

THEME VERSE

I will make those who are of the synagogue of Satan, who claim to be Jews
though they are not, but are liars—I will make them come and fall down
at your feet and acknowledge that I have loved you. (Revelation 3:9)

It might seem like I am here to preach to the choir—and maybe I am.
After all, there is little to fault you for as a congregation. Perhaps first I
should introduce myself. I am the angel Kleis *(Klay-iss)*, and my name
means "key." Jesus, whom I serve, holds the key to the New Jerusalem, a key
He has entrusted to the congregation here at Philadelphia and to every
Christian church. It's the key of the Gospel, a key that exists nowhere else
but in the church. Jesus' desire is that the Gospel key opens the way to
heaven. He sends you pastors to proclaim the Good News, even as Christ
commissioned the eleven remaining apostles after He rose. He poured His
Spirit out on them, they preached, and thousands entered into God's kingdom. The apostles baptized, and souls were washed clean, declared righteous before God. The apostles blessed bread and wine, and the body and
blood of Christ forgave, quickened, and strengthened the souls of the faithful. So it is among you. As you hear and receive the Good News, Jesus fills
you to overflowing, hearts are opened among your neighbors, whom you
love, and they are moved to believe in Christ Jesus.

That brings me to the purpose of my visit. I'm not here to tear you
down. You already have had enough of that, suffering as you have through
the frequent earthquakes that occur in your part of the world. If anything,
you who are living in such a dangerous city need reassurance of God's continued love. And He does love you. Your faithfulness in the face of trial,
temptation, and persecution is duly noted in heaven.

Your Christian brothers and sisters in neighboring towns would do well to follow your example. You face challenges similar to theirs, but when they have failed, you have stood firm. You have continued to trust God's Word and to believe in Jesus when it would be so much easier to return to paganism or Judaism.

This is a major wine-producing region. It would be tempting to join in the festivals for Dionysus, the wine god, known to the Romans as Bacchus. His cult is a powerful influence in Philadelphia. But the Jews, not the pagans, offer the most opposition to your faith—Jews who claim to be the rightful heirs of Abraham and David. They never cease trying to have you arrested on trumped up charges of disloyalty to Rome or practicing an illegal religion. Yet Christ came to the Jews first. He proclaimed the Good News of the kingdom to them. He did many miracles to prove His divinity, but the Jews spurned Him. They called for Jesus' death. Even after He rose from the dead, they refused to believe in Jesus. Here is the extent of their neglect: The Jews despised their birthright. They abandoned faith for dead works. So bitter and hateful has the antagonism from the Jews become that theirs is no longer a synagogue of God's people but a synagogue of Satan. They claim to be the true Israel, but the Lord Jesus calls them liars and children of the devil. That describes anyone in any religion who would turn away—or turn you away—from Jesus to false teachings. Woe to those who neglect the truth for error!

But don't hate the Jews. They are a synagogue of Satan only because the devil has blinded them to the truth. Pray that they will repent of their evil and learn that Jesus is the Son of David, the Messiah for whom they yearn. Deal kindly with them so on the day of Christ's return they may willingly, along with you, acknowledge Jesus as Savior rather than unwillingly bow to Him as judge.

Unlike the synagogue of Satan, your doctrine is pure. Your faith is strong. Your love for God's Word is unquestioned. Your morality is above reproach. Oh, that the other congregations were as you are! Once you were slaves of sin, living in guilt, having no hope because you were excluded from God's people and His promises of grace. You worshiped idols and chased after the vain and temporary things of this world. You once were as guilty of neglect as the unbelieving Jews. But when the key of Jesus' Gospel unlocked the gates of the kingdom of God for you, when you learned that He died and rose again for you, when you were baptized into Jesus, everything changed. "Once you were not a people, but now you are the people of God; once you had not received mercy, but now you have received mercy" (1 Peter 2:10).

You formerly blind pagans and rejected Gentiles are now "all sons of God through faith in Christ Jesus, for all of you who were baptized into Christ have clothed yourselves with Christ" (Galatians 3:26–27). You who had no status—women, slaves, non-Jews—all of you are now "Abraham's seed, and heirs" (Galatians 3:29). You are heirs of all the precious promises God made to Abraham and his descendants. All of this became your possession when you heard of Jesus, believed, and were baptized. All these treasures are opened through the key Christ has given to you.

Everyone, Jew and pagan, needs to hear of Jesus. The beloved apostle Paul has written: "For there is no difference between Jew and Gentile—the same Lord is Lord of all and richly blesses all who call on Him, for, 'Everyone who calls on the name of the Lord will be saved.' How, then, can they call on the one they have not believed in? And how can they believe in the one of whom they have not heard? And how can they hear without someone preaching to them? And how can they preach unless they are sent?" (Romans 10:12–15).

"I have placed before you an open door that no one can shut," the Lord Jesus says to you. "I know that you have little strength, yet you have kept My word and have not denied My name" (Revelation 3:8). "What open door?" you ask. Open doors come in all shapes, sizes, and places. One open door is assisting missionaries with your offerings. "How can they preach unless they are sent?" (Romans 10:15). And how can they be sent unless you give to support them? And there are other ways. You go to the market every day and meet neighbors and shopkeepers. In almost every conversation, someone will mention a need. That need—a frustration, a family problem, a regret, a worry—is the door through which Christ can enter when you speak a gentle word of faith. Needs exist all around you. People are sick, lonesome, hungry, poor, illiterate, confused, abandoned, dying. Every problem is an open door for Christ, whose love you can share with others by caring enough to help.

I am certain that you will use the key. To keep the word of Jesus and to confess Him is to proclaim Him. That is who you are, people who stand up for Jesus no matter how terrifying the adversary. You can do that, even in the face of persecution. "Hold on to what you have," the Lord Jesus encourages you (Revelation 3:11). Let no one take your crown. God will help you.

How do I know? Well, after all, I am an angel, and sometimes we angels are privy to information you do not ordinarily have. I happen to know that while great tribulation and suffering are about to come on you, you will bear up and continue to be faithful. There will be persecution from Rome that you cannot conceive of now, persecution far more horrible than the struggles you have with unbelieving Jews in Satan's synagogue. After Rome fades into history, you Christians in Philadelphia will withstand the onslaught of the Turks and Islam. Indeed, you will remain a free Christian city until well into the fourteenth century. Then, finally, the Turks will overwhelm you, but your faith and church will continue. Two thousand years from today, your descendants in Philadelphia will still honor the name of Jesus.

Jesus has the highest expectations of you, expectations that will be fulfilled not because of your strength but because of His. He will keep you strong in faith and love. In Baptism you were named God's child. Your name is written in the Book of Life. The promise of Jesus for you, and all who overcome, is that your names will be engraved on the pillars of the temple in heaven. Indeed, you will be the temple and Jesus Himself will live among you. It will be a temple unlike those here on earth, which are destroyed every few centuries by earthquakes. It will be a temple that lasts forever, safe from every enemy. This is Jesus' promise to you.

Christian friends, your city of Philadelphia is known as the "gate to Asia," situated as it is on a major highway. But your church, caretaker as it is of the Key of David, rests on the highway to the New Jerusalem. Use the key. Keep the gate open for every lost traveler who is seeking to find his or her way.

I Kleis, the key, am leaving your sight now, but not you, so do not be afraid. Although I can't really open doors for you, Christ can and does as you use the Gospel key of Word and Sacrament placed in your pastor's stewardship by Jesus so you might see heaven.

PRAYER

Gracious God, thank You for Jesus, the key to life, who has unlocked the door to heaven for me. Give me such love for others that I may freely share the key with them and so do my part, in Your strength, to carry out the Great Commission. In Jesus' name I pray. Amen.

LENT 5

CHILDREN'S SERMON

Revelation 3:7–13

VISUAL AID

Old-fashioned key ring with keys

THEME VERSE

These are the words of Him who is holy and true, who holds the key of David. What He opens no one can shut, and what He shuts no one can open. (Revelation 3:7)

Hello, children. It is so good to see you back. I am looking forward to Palm Sunday and, after that, Easter, the day we celebrate the resurrection of Jesus. When Jesus rose from the dead, He unlocked the graves of all who love Him so they might live forever with Him in heaven.

I would like to show you some keys I have hanging on my wall. These are old-fashioned brass keys on a big key ring. Would you like to look at them? *(Allow the children to pass around the keys.)* Keys like these once fit in big locks on heavy doors. If the door was locked, you could not get in unless you had the key.

Did you know that to get into heaven you need the right key? *(Allow children to respond.)* Heaven is a perfect place where there is no sin, suffering, or evil. There is no one in heaven but God, the holy angels, and holy people. You and I are sinners who do not deserve to get into heaven, but we can enter heaven if we have the right key. What do you think the key is? *(Allow children to respond. Some might answer "the cross" or "Jesus.")*

Yes, the key to heaven is Jesus and His cross. Through God's gifts in Baptism and His Word, we believe in Jesus and have the key to heaven. It is the most precious treasure we have. But it is not a treasure we want to keep locked up. We want to share it. When we tell other people that Jesus loves them, that He died for their sins, and that He rose from the dead, we are offering them the key to heaven.

74

Wouldn't it be wonderful if everyone knew about Jesus' love and had the key of faith so they could be in heaven too? With whom could you share the key? *(Allow children to respond.)* Let's pray that God will help us tell others about Jesus so they can have the key to heaven too.

PRAYER

Dear Lord Jesus, You hold the key to heaven and You have given it to me. Because You died for my sins and rose again, I have a home with You forever. Help me share the key with my family and friends. Give them faith to take the key. In Your holy name I pray. Amen.

LENT 6

THE LETTER TO LAODICEA: COMPLACENCY—DEATH BY INDIFFERENCE

Amos 6:1–7; Revelation 3:14–22; John 15:9–17

THEME VERSE

So, because you are lukewarm—neither hot nor cold—I am about to spit
you out of My mouth. (Revelation 3:16)

Listen up! I am Martus, an angel on special assignment from the Lord
Jesus Christ to your church. I wish there were a nice way for me to tell
you this, but there isn't. So I will be blunt. The Lord Jesus is disgusted with
you. He is nauseated to the point of vomiting. There, I have said it.

The apostle John has given me a letter from Christ that I will share with
you. It outlines the reasons for our Lord's displeasure. You wonder why He
is upset. After all, your congregation at Laodicea is the picture of success.
Your community is thriving, situated as it is at the intersection of several
major trade routes. You are the provincial capital. The black wool from
your sheep and the woven garments you make are widely sought after. You
have a famous medical school, as well as a temple to the god of healing.
Ointments for curing diseases of the eyes and ears are made in Laodicea.
Emperor worship has reached your city and continues to grow in popular-
ity. Prosperous, educated, religious, important—no wonder so many people
want to live in Laodicea.

As a congregation, you seem not to be plagued with the moral and doctrinal troubles of your sister congregations. One could not describe you as
idolatrous or immoral or tempted to compromise the Christian faith. In
fact, a visitor to your church might remark, "What a lovely congregation
and what nice people. How prosperous and peaceful things seem." Even the
name of your city, Laodicea, might imply that you are a people of righteousness.

There is only one problem, one deadly flaw. You are so self-satisfied that you have no use for Christ. He is everything, yet to you, Christ is nothing. He is the "Amen," the only certainty, yet your certainty lies within yourselves. He is the faithful and true witness, the martyr, which is the origin of my name, Martus. Christ died to save you from every evil and give you His righteousness, and you think you have done it yourselves. Christ is the source of all creation, without whom nothing would exist, and you have the gall to pat yourselves on the back and say, "We did it all ourselves." You smile smugly at your good fortune and say, "I am rich; I have acquired wealth and do not need a thing" (Revelation 3:17). And you wonder why Jesus is about to throw up! You neither love Him nor despise Him; you neither call on Him nor send Him away.

You remind me of the rich farmer in Jesus' parable. His ground produced such a huge crop that he had no place to store it. So he pulled down his old barns and built bigger ones, telling himself, "I have plenty of good things laid up for many years. I'll take life easy; eat, drink and be merry" (Luke 12:19). But God said to him, "You fool! This very night your life will be demanded from you" (Luke 12:20). The farmer went to bed complacent, satisfied, selfish. He woke up damned to hell.

Laodicea, this is not what God wants for you. Repent! Come back to Jesus! You think you are rich, but you are poor in what matters: humility and faith. You think you can see because of your fine doctors and your eye medications, but you are blind to your own sin and helplessness. You think that because you are dressed in the finest woolens your craftspeople can make that you are clothed. But without Christ you are naked of any righteousness, shameful in your sins.

Repent! Come back to Jesus! Don't you realize that you are destitute of all you think you have? Those things you boast of now are but a passing illusion of well-being. Jesus, the only certainty, Jesus, the source of all creation, has come to meet your needs with real treasure. Through His victory over Satan, Jesus has won for you the golden streets of heaven. Through His blood spilled at Calvary, Jesus has won for you the white garments of His righteousness. Through His Holy Spirit, Jesus has taken away the blindness of your soul, enabling you to see His glory, glory that makes all else pale in comparison.

Christ's words to you have been harsh, difficult for me to say, and difficult for you to accept. But they are spoken in love. The Lord Jesus says,

"Those whom I love I rebuke and discipline" (Revelation 3:19). If He did not love you, He would not have died for you. If He did not love you, He would not have sent missionaries and pastors to share His Gospel with you. If He did not love you, He would not have made you His children in Holy Baptism. If He did not love you, He would not invite you to pray "Our Father in heaven." If He did not love you, He would not have inspired an old man who is suffering on an island to write you this letter. If He did not love you, He would not have sent me, His angel, to bring you this message, begging you to repent and return to Him. If He did not love you, He would not care a whit about the danger you face. But He does care.

Jesus loves you. He died for you. This is His church. He says to you, His blood-bought people, "Here I am! I stand at the door and knock. If anyone hears My voice and opens the door, I will come in and eat with him, and he with Me" (Revelation 3:20).

Jesus is knocking now. He is calling this congregation, each member of this congregation, by name. Soon you will be celebrating His Holy Supper. You will break bread and pour wine. You'll repeat the words "This is My body" and "This is My blood," given and shed for you for the forgiveness of sins. This is a means of grace for you. Here you find the forgiveness of sins, including your sin of apathy. Now, before the Holy Meal, is the time to remember Christ who has always committed Himself to you. As St. Paul tells you, now, before you eat of the bread and drink of the cup, is the time for self-examination.

Today Jesus calls you to admit again to yourself and to God your sin and helplessness. Recognize that no good thing, despite all the trappings of success, dwells in you. Acknowledge that all you have and are comes not of your own effort but from God. Repent of your lukewarm faith. As you do, the Holy Spirit, by means of the Word and Sacraments, will set a fire within you, moving you to bold acts that confess God's love for you, reflect your love for God, and pour out God's love and the Gospel on your neighbor.

As you repent, you will lose nothing but your sin and guilt. In their place will be a peace of mind and heart as fresh as a spring morning after the rain. You will gain precious promises from Jesus: "To him who overcomes, I will give the right to sit with Me on My throne, just as I overcame and sat down with My Father on His throne" (Revelation 3:21). But you will have nothing to boast about because the victory that gains the throne of heaven has been won for you by Jesus and becomes yours by faith. Don't delay!

So what will Laodicea do? Some of you will heed your Lord's call. Two-and-a-half centuries from now, your church will still be here, moderately important, led by your own bishop. A church council will meet here to publish a document called "The Canons of Laodicea." In its sixty chapters, you will make pronouncements about various heresies, when to celebrate Easter, the proper form of the liturgy, and how to observe Lent. You will even offer a list of all the books you feel should be included in the Bible—though you will not mention the Book of Revelation and its Letter to Laodicea.

I have done my part, given my witness to the word of Christ as my name, Martus, calls me to do. I had better be going because the temperature seems to be rising in here. It could be the flush that follows a justified rebuke, or, as I pray it is, the Holy Spirit is kindling a renewed flame of faith in your hearts.

PRAYER

Lord Jesus, I admit my complacency, my self-satisfied attitude, my lack of love for You and my neighbor. Forgive me and rekindle in my heart the fire of Your Holy Spirit. In Your holy name I pray. Amen.

LENT 6

CHILDREN'S SERMON

Revelation 3:14–22

VISUAL AIDS

Open can of soda, warm and without fizz
Small paper drinking cups

THEME VERSE

So, because you are lukewarm—neither hot nor cold—I am about to spit
you out of My mouth. (Revelation 3:16)

It is Holy Week at last. This is a happy and a sad week, isn't it? *(Allow children to respond.)* It is sad because this is the week we remember in a special way the suffering and death of Jesus for our sins. But it is happy because Jesus rose from the dead on Easter morning. That makes me feel so much better.

Are you thirsty? *(Allow children to respond.)* Who would like a cup of soda? *(Acknowledge that most of the children have raised their hands.)* I will pour a cup. *(Select one or two children to receive cups of soda.)* Now, let's drink. *(Take a sip and make sure the children do too.)* Why are you making a terrible face? *(Allow children to explain what is wrong.)* Yes, the soda is warm, and it doesn't have any fizz. It tastes terrible, doesn't it? *(Allow children to respond.)*

That is how Jesus describes people who claim to be Christians but do not seem to care about loving God or their neighbor. They might go to church, but they find Jesus and the Christian life boring. It doesn't make any difference to them that Jesus died on the cross and rose again so they might have eternal life. They do not really care whether anyone else hears the story of God's love in Jesus.

How sad it is to think some people feel this way about Jesus. Jesus thinks it is sad, too, especially because He loves everyone so much. He would much rather a person be hot or cold than lukewarm in their faith. Lukewarm is disgusting. But when someone is hot or cold in their faith, at least you know whether they are on Jesus' side.

Are you on Jesus' side? Is your faith hot with love for Jesus? *(Allow children to respond.)* I pray that you have a red-hot faith. I am glad you have come to church because this is where we learn from God's Word about Jesus and His love and where the spark of faith can become a flame. That is what we want. Let's pray that the Holy Spirit will help our faith be hot for Jesus.

PRAYER

Holy Spirit, give me the fire of faith in Jesus. Make me useful to Jesus and my neighbor. Help me to keep trusting in the cross of Jesus and His resurrection so I will know my sins are forgiven and I have a home with Him in heaven. In His name I pray. Amen.

EASTER

Come, Take Your Crown!

Revelation 2:8–11

Theme Verse

These are the words of Him who is the First and the Last, who died and came to life again. (Revelation 2:8b)

Some time ago, a father contacted the pastor of his church with wonderful news. The pretty and intelligent elementary-school daughter of this poor family had been nominated to participate in a Little Princess pageant. The family was excited because if this young girl won the crown, she would bring home fabulous prizes: a new car, a family trip to Disney World, a full scholarship to the university of her choice. The parents were sure she would win because their daughter was smart, attractive, and talented.

There was a problem, however. To enter the pageant, the family had to come up with thousands of dollars in fees. The pastor smelled a rat. It had to be a scam because only days before another family with little money had told him their son had been nominated to participate in a Little Prince pageant. How cruel! Someone was profiting by targeting poor families who wanted things to be better in their lives. These families dreamed of a crown that would bring a new life, but the reality was a scam.

We do not have to settle for scams. Christ has won for us a crown: a new life, a rich and happy life—indeed, eternal life. Christ promises this to all who know Him by faith. That is the good news the angel brings from Jesus to the church at Smyrna: "These are the words of Him who is the First and the Last, who died and came to life again" (Revelation 2:8). That is the good news the angel brings to us today. The crucified and risen Savior you have believed in is eternal. He has always been and will always be. And you are safe in Christ, no matter what.

Jesus as the First and the Last is something like a set of bookends. Above my desk is a shelf on which I keep the books I use most often. There are only about a dozen. I have hundreds of others, but those above my desk are the ones most precious to me. Some are big and heavy. Some are thin and flimsy. By themselves these books tend to fall over like dominoes, hitting the floor, breaking their bindings. To keep them safe, I push them together and prop them up with bookends, one heavy brass bookend on each end of the shelf. Between the bookends my books are secure.

You and I are secure in Jesus, the First and the Last, who died and lives. Like bookends, this great truth of faith is seen at the beginning of our Christian life and at the end. In Holy Baptism we have our new birth. In this washing, the eternal Son of God, who died for our sins but now lives, sends us His Holy Spirit, breathing into us new life and a new nature. We are washed clean. We are given the righteousness of Christ. We are given faith to receive His gifts. Then, blessed with however many days and years God gives us on this earth, we die and are buried. But the power of new life in Baptism goes on. The body made holy in the Sacrament of Baptism is kept safe until the day of resurrection. On that day it comes forth, wondrously new and whole, never to suffer or die again. Jesus, the First and the Last, who died and lives, guarantees this with His cross and empty tomb and our Baptism. This is the crown that matters, the certainty of every believer.

Nearly 2,000 years ago, the Christians at Smyrna believed this. You and I believe this. This is why so many of us have gathered today in celebration. As we sing in the hymn: "Jesus lives! The vict'ry's won! Death no longer can appall me!" (*Lutheran Worship*, 139:1). We know the first part of this beloved hymn verse is true. It is the second part with which we have problems. We are absolutely convinced that the crown of life is ours, but there are so many frightening things that stand between us and that glorious day when we will receive this crown.

That was the experience of the church at Smyrna. Christianity was not a legal religion. It was okay to be a pagan or a Jew but not a Christian. One could worship at any of the temples of the local pagan gods; one could worship Rome, the emperor, or the Roman Senate; one could attend the synagogue, but Christians were suspect. They served a different king. They might be accused of cannibalism because their worship services included eating and drinking the body and blood of Christ. In the eyes of some, because Christians did not worship a statue of their God, they did not really have a god, which meant they were atheists, and atheists were undesirable.

Because Christianity was not legal, Christians were persecuted. The pagans would accuse Christians of disloyalty to the emperor. After all, if they were loyal, they would worship the emperor's image like everyone else. The Jews, whose religion was protected, would make it clear that Christians were not part of the synagogue. Christian merchants had trouble selling their goods to pagans and Jews. Without ties to the community, Christians often had difficulty finding work. Some Christians were extremely poor; some faced starvation. Those that didn't starve might be arrested and killed unless they denied their faith. This happened to Smyrna's most famous pastor, Polycarp. He died for his faith rather than deny Jesus.

The Christians in Smyrna had to endure persecution. They also had to contend with the temptations that come from the world, the devil, and our sinful nature. And bad things happened—injuries, illness, accidents, death—to test these Christians. But in all these things, the Christians of Smyrna found a gracious God in Jesus Christ, a God nearby and not far off, a God who walked with them and suffered with them.

Let's move the clock ahead to our day. If you believe in Jesus Christ and bad things are happening to you, you might wonder where the promised crown is. You might even be tempted to fall away from Jesus if things become bad enough. And things can become pretty bad. You do not have to live in first-century Smyrna to suffer and wonder whether Jesus loves you. For example:

- A 22-year-old man suffers from kidney failure. He is on dialysis and may die unless someone donates a kidney.

- An elderly woman sells her home and moves in with a relative in what is supposed to be a mutually beneficial arrangement. A few months later, the relative throws her out and the woman is homeless.

- A young couple rejoices at the news they will have their first baby. A few months later, the doctor tells them their unborn baby does not have a brain.

- A faithful father and husband who has successfully supported his family for years finds himself unemployed—and remains unemployed one year later.

- A middle-age woman—attractive, faithful in her marriage, active in church—is dumped by her husband after an anniversary trip to Hawaii. He has found a younger woman.

Maybe you have your own examples of suffering endured by Christians. Maybe you are in the middle of some painful experience you haven't told anyone about. When suffering happens to faithful Christians—Christians at Smyrna, Christians in this church today—we wonder why. What did this person do—what did I do—to deserve this? We might ask the Lord if He is punishing us. The answer is a loud and clear no. God is not punishing us. All we have to do to be assured of this answer is look to Jesus and the cross on which He died. To all who turn toward the cross, Jesus says: "I am your Savior, and I have died here for your sins—all of them. I took the punishment your sins deserved, and I give you My forgiveness and righteousness in exchange. How could you possibly think I'm punishing you? If that were true, I died for nothing. But I live! I am not the cause of your suffering; I am the solution." That is the message of Jesus and His cross.

Why do we suffer? Why did the Christians at Smyrna suffer? Suffering happens so we might know God's faithfulness. God is not the author or cause of evil or any bad thing that happens, the devil is. But as Luther says, the devil is God's devil. That means the devil can only do as much evil as God allows him to do. And in his wisdom, God sometimes allows the devil to do a measured amount of evil so good may result. Think of Jesus' death. The devil tempted Judas to betray Jesus. The devil convinced men to condemn Jesus to death. The events of Jesus' passion were bad. His death was unjust. But the result was the redemption of humanity.

The devil tested some Christians at Smyrna with prison and some, such as their pastor, Polycarp, with death. But suffering is always limited. It is just long enough and intense enough for those who experience it to learn that God keeps His promises. Christ has bound the devil and keeps him on a chain (Revelation 20:1–3). Christ says: "I tell you, the devil will put some of you in prison to test you, and you will suffer persecution for ten days" (Revelation 2:10). Whatever the pain, the heartbreak, the persecution, it lasts for only ten days. It is limited. It is brief. As Paul says: "No temptation has seized you except what is common to man. And God is faithful; He will not let you be tempted beyond what you can bear. But when you are tempted, He will also provide a way out so that you can stand up under it" (1 Corinthians 10:13). In fact, testing is nothing at all when compared to the blessings of the crown of life. With the crown of life guaranteed by the one who "died and came to life again," we can get through the testing. In Christ we have the victory.

That is the promise found in Jesus' words to the Christians of Smyrna and to us. Because Jesus died and lives again, our crown of life is certain.

Revelation 2:10 says literally in the Greek: "Believe this until death, and I will give you the wreath of life." This is sports terminology. It is a picture of what the future holds for the winning athlete. The athlete trains, exercises, runs, spars with opponents, pours all his or her energy and strength into the competition. Why? For that moment of glory when the grand marshal of the games welcomes the winner to the victor's circle to award the laurel wreath while the crowd cheers.

But there is a difference between athletic competitions and the contest in which we Christians are involved. In athletics, victory or defeat depends on personal effort, how hard one pushes oneself. Also there is only one winner, and everyone else loses. But in the contest that leads to the crown of life, the winner already has been crowned, and the winner is Jesus. He has defeated the opponent. Satan is crushed at the cross and the empty tomb. You and I share the victor's crown with Jesus not because of our personal efforts but by faith—faith that is given and sustained by Word and Sacraments. Believe this, even to the point of death, and Jesus will give you the crown of life.

I was serving Communion at a retirement home to a group of residents, one of whom was Annie, a 106-year-old woman. Each of the previous times I had seen Annie, her hair and makeup had been perfect. She typically wore a beautiful dress adorned with a corsage. As she entered the room set aside for the service on this particular visit, things were different. There was no flower nor makeup. Although she was in a wheelchair, Annie still wore a beautiful smile. Instead of asking about my family as she usually did, Annie repeated again and again, "You know, I'm going to die soon."

Initially, I felt like changing the subject or saying, "Oh, Annie, you'll be with us for a long time yet." But I let her continue her mantra. Then I realized that Annie considered this to be a happy announcement. She had been faithful. Now she was near death, and she was still smiling. She was about to see Jesus. Annie was going to receive her crown of life. I smiled too.

Prayer

Lord Jesus, You are the First and the Last. You died and now You live again. By Your Word and Sacraments, keep us always in faith so we might leave this world with joy and receive the crown of life You have won for us. In Your name we pray. Amen.

EASTER

CHILDREN'S SERMON

Revelation 2:10

VISUAL AID

Athlete's wreath made of vines or flowers

THEME VERSE

Be faithful, even to the point of death, and I will give you the crown of life. (Revelation 2:10)

Good morning, children. Who can tell me what today is? *(Allow children to respond.)* Yes, today is Easter. It is the day we rejoice that Jesus is alive. I am going to teach you the Easter greeting. I say "He is risen!" and you respond "He is risen, indeed!" Let's try it. *(Repeat the greeting until the children know it.)*

What do you think of my crown? *(Allow children to hold and touch the wreath.)* Would someone like to wear it? *(Put the wreath on a child's head.)* Although it is not made of silver or gold, it is valuable. In ancient times, an athlete would receive a wreath like this when he won a race. He would spend all his time and energy working out and practicing to win this crown and the honor that went with it. How long do you think a crown like this might last? *(Allow children to respond.)* Right, probably not long. The leaves and flowers eventually will wilt, dry up, and turn to dust.

Did you know Jesus has a crown for you? He does, but it is not a crown like this wreath. It is a crown that lasts forever. It is the crown of life. Jesus died for our sins and lives again so we do not have to be afraid of dying. All who are baptized into Jesus and believe in Him share in His life. Although we die, we continue living with Him in heaven and one day our old bodies will become wonderful new bodies like Jesus' body. That is the crown of life Jesus is going to give to you and me. I am looking forward to that day, aren't you? Let's pray.

Prayer

Thank You, Lord Jesus, that You died for my sins and rose again. Give me faith that I might always know I am forgiven and have a crown of life with You in heaven. In Your name I pray. Amen.

ORDERS OF SERVICE

ASH WEDNESDAY

LOVE LOST, DEATH FOUND

(*Stand for silent procession of the cross*)

HYMN: "A MIGHTY FORTRESS IS OUR GOD"
(*Lutheran Worship* 297, stanzas 1–2)

PSALM 98:1–3

P: Sing to the LORD a new song, for He has done marvelous things;

C: HIS RIGHT HAND AND HIS HOLY ARM HAVE WORKED SALVATION FOR HIM.

P: The LORD has made His salvation known and revealed His righteousness to the nations.

ALL: He has remembered His love and His faithfulness to the house of Israel; all the ends of the earth have seen the salvation of our God.

HYMN: "A MIGHTY FORTRESS IS OUR GOD"
(*Lutheran Worship*, 297, stanzas 3–4)

THE CONFESSIONAL SERVICE WITH IMPOSITION OF ASHES
(*Lutheran Worship*, p. 308)
(*Be seated*)

THE FIRST LESSON

Genesis 3:21–23 "God banished him from the garden."

L: This is the Word of the Lord.

C: THANKS BE TO GOD.

THE EPISTLE LESSON

Revelation 2:1–7 "You have forsaken your first love."

L: This is what the Spirit says to the churches. (Revelation 2:11)

C: THANKS BE TO GOD.

THE HOLY GOSPEL

John 15:9–17 "He lay down his life for his friends."

(*Stand*)

P: This is the Gospel of the Lord.

C: PRAISE TO YOU, O CHRIST.

(*Be seated*)

THE CHILDREN'S SERMON

HYMN: "I LOVE YOUR KINGDOM, LORD" (*Lutheran Worship*, 296)

THE SERMON

The Letter to Ephesus: Love Lost, Death Found

(*Stand*)

THE NICENE CREED

(*Be seated*)

THE OFFERING

(*Stand*)

THE PRAYER OF THE DAY

ALL: O Jesus, Lord of the church, I am in danger every day of leaving You, my first love. Deliver and protect me from all that threatens my faith. Give me courage to overcome temptation. Help me to trust You daily that I might ever eat from the tree of life in the paradise of God. In Your holy name, I pray. Amen.

The Pastoral Prayers

P: Lord, in Your mercy

C: HEAR US, O LORD.

THE LORD'S PRAYER

SERVICE OF HOLY COMMUNION

(*Be seated for Communion distribution*)

DISTRIBUTION HYMNS

    "I Lay My Sins on Jesus" (*Lutheran Worship*, 366)

    "Lord of Glory, You Have Bought Us" (*Lutheran Worship*, 402)

(*Stand*)

THE BENEDICTION

P: He who has an ear, let him hear what the Spirit says to the churches. (Revelation 2:7)

C: TO HIM WHO OVERCOMES, I WILL GIVE THE RIGHT TO EAT FROM THE TREE OF LIFE, WHICH IS THE PARADISE OF GOD. (Revelation 2:7)

P: The grace of the Lord Jesus be with God's people. In the name of the Father and of the + Son and of the Holy Spirit.

C: AMEN.

(*Silent recession of the cross*)

LENTEN WORSHIP 1

FEAR UNTO DEATH VS. COURAGE UNTO LIFE

(*Stand*)

THE INVOCATION

P: In the name of the Father and of the + Son and of the Holy Spirit.

C: AMEN.

HYMN: "WHAT A FRIEND WE HAVE IN JESUS"
(*Lutheran Worship*, 516, stanzas 1–2)

PSALM 16:1–6

P: Keep me safe, O God, for in You I take refuge.

C: I SAID TO THE LORD, "YOU ARE MY LORD; APART FROM YOU I HAVE NO GOOD THING."

P: As for the saints who are in the land, they are the glorious ones in whom is all my delight.

C: THE SORROWS OF THOSE WILL INCREASE WHO RUN AFTER OTHER GODS. I WILL NOT POUR OUT THEIR LIBATIONS OF BLOOD OR TAKE UP THEIR NAMES ON MY LIPS.

P: LORD, You have assigned me my portion and my cup; You have made my lot secure.

ALL: The boundary lines have fallen for me in pleasant places; surely I have a delightful inheritance.

HYMN: "WHAT A FRIEND WE HAVE IN JESUS"
(*Lutheran Worship*, 516, stanza 3)

(*Be seated*)

THE FIRST LESSON

Isaiah 14:12–17 "Is this the man who shook the earth?"

L: This is the Word of the Lord.

C: THANKS BE TO GOD.

THE EPISTLE LESSON

Revelation 2:8–11 "Do not be afraid of what you are about to suffer."

P: This is what the Spirit says to the churches. (Revelation 2:11)

C: THANKS BE TO GOD.

THE HOLY GOSPEL

Matthew 24:4–15 "See to it that you are not alarmed."

(*Stand*)

P: This is the Gospel of the Lord.

C: PRAISE TO YOU, O CHRIST.

(*Be seated*)

THE CHILDREN'S SERMON

Hymn: "The Lord's My Shepherd, I'll Not Want"
(*Lutheran Worship*, 416)

THE SERMON

The Letter to Smyrna: Fear unto Death vs. Courage unto Life

(*Stand*)

THE APOSTLES' CREED

(*Be seated*)

THE OFFERING

(*Stand*)

THE PRAYER OF THE DAY

ALL: O Jesus, risen Savior, my enemies of mind and body often frighten me. Assure me that because you died and overcame death, nothing can separate me from the crown of life You have won for me and all believers. Enable me to live boldly each day for You. In Your holy name I pray. Amen.

THE PASTORAL PRAYERS

P: Lord, in Your mercy

C: HEAR OUR PRAYER.

THE LORD'S PRAYER

THE BENEDICTION

P: He who has an ear, let him hear what the Spirit says to the churches. (Revelation 2:11)

C: HE WHO OVERCOMES WILL NOT BE HURT AT ALL BY THE SECOND DEATH. (Revelation 2:11)

P: The grace of the Lord Jesus be with God's people. In the name of the Father and of the + Son and of the Holy Spirit.

C: AMEN.

CLOSING HYMN: "IN THE HOUR OF TRIAL" (*Lutheran Worship*, 511)

LENTEN WORSHIP 2

IDOLATRY IS THE DEADLIEST SIN

(*Stand*)

THE INVOCATION

P: In the name of the Father and of the + Son and of the Holy Spirit.

C: AMEN.

HYMN: "COME, O ALMIGHTY KING"
(*Lutheran Worship*, 169, stanzas 1–2)

PSALM 78:1, 19–20, 23–25, 32, 38

P: O My people, hear My teaching; listen to the words of My mouth. "Can God spread a table in the desert? . . . Can He supply meat for His people?"

C: YET HE GAVE A COMMAND TO THE SKIES ABOVE AND OPENED THE DOORS OF THE HEAVENS; HE RAINED DOWN MANNA FOR THE PEOPLE TO EAT . . . . MEN ATE THE BREAD OF ANGELS.

P: In spite of all this, they kept on sinning; in spite of His wonders, they did not believe.

ALL: Yet He was merciful; He forgave their iniquities and did not destroy them.

HYMN: "COME, O ALMIGHTY KING" (*Lutheran Worship*, 169, stanzas 3–4)
(*Be seated*)

THE FIRST LESSON

Numbers 22:1–20 "Come and put a curse on these people."

L: This is the Word of the Lord.

C: THANKS BE TO GOD.

THE EPISTLE LESSON

Revelation 2:12–17 "To him who overcomes, I will give some of the hidden manna."

L: This is what the Spirit says to the churches. (Revelation 2:17)

C: THANKS BE TO GOD.

THE HOLY GOSPEL

John 6:26–33 "The bread of God is He who comes down from heaven."

(*Stand*)

P: This is the Gospel of the Lord.

C: PRAISE TO YOU, O CHRIST.

(*Be seated*)

THE CHILDREN'S SERMON

HYMN: "HOW PRECIOUS IS THE BOOK DIVINE" (*Lutheran Worship*, 332)

THE SERMON

The Letter to Pergamum: Idolatry Is the Deadliest Sin

(*Stand*)

THE APOSTLES' CREED

(*Be seated*)

THE OFFERING

(*Stand*)

THE PRAYER OF THE DAY

ALL: Jesus, coming Judge, let me never be led astray by the lure of money or false teaching. Instead, enable me always to listen to Your Spirit speaking through Your Word so I may be found faithful when You come. In Your name I pray. Amen.

THE PASTORAL PRAYERS

P: Lord, in Your mercy

C: HEAR OUR PRAYER.

THE LORD'S PRAYER

THE BENEDICTION

P: He who has an ear, let him hear what the Spirit says to the churches. (Revelation 2:17)

C: TO HIM WHO OVERCOMES, I WILL GIVE SOME OF THE HIDDEN MANNA. (Revelation 2:17)

P: The grace of our Lord Jesus be with God's people. In the name of the Father and of the + Son and of the Holy Spirit

C: AMEN.

CLOSING HYMN: "O WORD OF GOD INCARNATE" (*Lutheran Worship*, 335)

LENTEN WORSHIP 3

IMMORALITY, HIGHWAY TO THE GRAVE

(*Stand*)

THE INVOCATION

P: In the name of the Father and of the + Son and of the Holy Spirit.
C: AMEN.

HYMN: "ALL GLORY BE TO GOD ON HIGH"
(*Lutheran Worship*, 215, stanzas 1–2)

PSALM 7:8, 9–10, 17

P: Let the LORD judge the peoples.

C: O RIGHTEOUS GOD, WHO SEARCHES MINDS AND HEARTS, BRING TO AN END THE VIOLENCE OF THE WICKED AND MAKE THE RIGHTEOUS SECURE.

P: My shield is God Most High, who saves the upright in heart.

ALL: I will give thanks to the LORD because of His righteousness and will sing praise to the name of the LORD Most High.

HYMN: "ALL GLORY BE TO GOD ON HIGH"
(*Lutheran Worship*, 215, stanzas 3–4)

(*Be seated*)

THE FIRST LESSON

1 Kings 16:29–33 "(Ahab) . . . married Jezebel."

L: This is the Word of the Lord.
C: THANKS BE TO GOD.

THE EPISTLE LESSON

Revelation 2:18–29 "You tolerate that woman Jezebel."

L: This is the Word of the Lord.
C: THANKS BE TO GOD.

The Holy Gospel

Matthew 25:31–46 "He will put the sheep on His right and the goats on His left."

(*Stand*)

P: This is the Gospel of the Lord.

C: PRAISE TO YOU, O CHRIST.

(*Be seated*)

THE CHILDREN'S SERMON

HYMN: "LORD JESUS, THINK ON ME" (*Lutheran Worship*, 231)

THE SERMON

The Letter to Thyatira: Immorality, Highway to the Grave

(*Stand*)

THE APOSTLES' CREED

(*Be seated*)

THE OFFERING

(*Stand*)

THE PRAYER OF THE DAY

ALL: Jesus, Son of God, You know my faith, my love, my service, what I have done, and what I have not done. Grant me discernment of good and evil so nothing false might deceive me and lead me away from true righteousness, which is Your gift to me. In Your name I pray. Amen.

THE PASTORAL PRAYERS

P: Lord, in Your mercy

C: HEAR OUR PRAYER.

THE LORD'S PRAYER

THE BENEDICTION

P: To him who overcomes and does My will to the end, (Revelation 2:26)

C: I WILL ALSO GIVE HIM THE MORNING STAR. HE WHO HAS AN EAR, LET HIM HEAR WHAT THE SPIRIT SAYS TO THE CHURCHES. (Revelation 2:28–29)

P: The grace of the Lord Jesus be with God's people. In the name of the Father and of the + Son and of the Holy Spirit.

C: AMEN.

CLOSING HYMN: "THE DAY IS SURELY DRAWING NEAR"
(*Lutheran Worship*, 462)

LENTEN WORSHIP 4

LETHARGY—SLOW DEATH

(*Stand*)

THE INVOCATION

P: In the name of the Father and of the + Son and of the Holy Spirit.

C: AMEN.

HYMN: "LORD, KEEP US STEADFAST IN YOUR WORD" (*Lutheran Worship,* 334, stanza 1)

PSALM 139:1–4, 11–12, 23–24

P: O LORD, You have searched me and You know me.

C: YOU KNOW WHEN I SIT AND WHEN I RISE; YOU PERCEIVE MY THOUGHTS FROM AFAR.

P: You discern my going out and my lying down; You are familiar with all my ways.

C: BEFORE A WORD IS ON MY TONGUE YOU KNOW IT COMPLETELY, O LORD.

P: If I say, "Surely the darkness will hide me and the light become night around me,"

C: EVEN THE DARKNESS WILL NOT BE DARK TO YOU; THE NIGHT WILL SHINE LIKE THE DAY, FOR DARKNESS IS AS LIGHT TO YOU.

P: Search me, O God, and know my heart; test me and know my anxious thoughts.

ALL: See if there is any offensive way in me, and lead me in the way everlasting.

HYMN: "LORD, KEEP US STEADFAST IN YOUR WORD" (*Lutheran Worship,* 334, stanzas 2–3)

(*Be seated*)

THE FIRST LESSON

Isaiah 29:13–16 "These people . . . honor Me with their lips but their hearts are far from Me."

L: This is the Word of the Lord.

C: THANKS BE TO GOD.

THE EPISTLE LESSON

Revelation 3:1–6 "Wake up! Strengthen what remains."

L: This is the Word of the Lord.

C: THANKS BE TO GOD.

THE HOLY GOSPEL

Matthew 24:42–51 "Keep watch, because you do not know on what day your Lord will come."

(*Stand*)

P: This is the Gospel of the Lord.

C: PRAISE TO YOU, O CHRIST.

(*Be seated*)

THE CHILDREN'S SERMON

HYMN: "RISE, MY SOUL, TO WATCH AND PRAY" (*Lutheran Worship*, 302)

THE SERMON

The Letter to Sardis: Lethargy—Slow Death

(*Stand*)

THE APOSTLES' CREED

(*Be seated*)

THE OFFERING

(*Stand*)

THE PRAYER OF THE DAY

ALL: Lord Jesus, coming Judge, keep me ever watchful that I might not stain my garments with sin. Through Your Word and Spirit, perfect holiness in my life that the Last Day may find me prepared through repentance and faith. In Your name I pray. Amen.

THE PASTORAL PRAYERS

P: Lord, in Your mercy

C: HEAR US, O LORD.

THE LORD'S PRAYER

THE BENEDICTION

P: He who overcomes will . . . be dressed in white. I will never blot out his name from the book of life,

C: BUT WILL ACKNOWLEDGE HIS NAME BEFORE MY FATHER AND HIS ANGELS. HE WHO HAS AN EAR, LET HIM HEAR WHAT THE SPIRIT SAYS TO THE CHURCHES. (Revelation 3:5)

P: The grace of the Lord Jesus be with God's people. In the name of the Father and of the + Son and of the Holy Spirit

C: AMEN.

CLOSING HYMN: "OH, THAT THE LORD WOULD GUIDE MY WAYS" (*Lutheran Worship*, 392)

LENTEN WORSHIP 5

NEGLECT—LOCKED OUT IN DEATH'S NIGHT

(*Stand*)

THE INVOCATION

P: In the name of the Father and of the + Son and of the Holy Spirit.

C: **AMEN.**

HYMN: "O HOLY SPIRIT, ENTER IN" (*Lutheran Worship*, 160, stanza 1)

PSALM 132:11, 13–18

P: The LORD swore an oath to David, a sure oath that He will not revoke:

C: **"ONE OF YOUR OWN DESCENDANTS I WILL PLACE ON YOUR THRONE."**

P: For the LORD has chosen Zion, He has desired it for His dwelling:

C: **"THIS IS MY RESTING PLACE FOR EVER AND EVER; HERE I WILL SIT ENTHRONED, FOR I HAVE DESIRED IT—**

P: I will bless her with abundant provisions; her poor will I satisfy with food.

C: **I WILL CLOTHE HER PRIESTS WITH SALVATION, AND HER SAINTS WILL EVER SING FOR JOY.**

P: Here I will make a horn grow for David and set up a lamp for My Anointed One.

ALL: I will clothe His enemies with shame, but the crown on His head will be resplendent."

HYMN: "O HOLY SPIRIT, ENTER IN" (*Lutheran Worship*, 160, stanzas 2–3)

(*Be seated*)

THE FIRST LESSON

Isaiah 60:3–11 "Nations will come to Your light."

L: This is the Word of the Lord.

C: THANKS BE TO GOD.

THE EPISTLE LESSON

Revelation 3:7–13 "I have placed before you an open door."

L: This is the Word of the Lord.

C: THANKS BE TO GOD.

THE HOLY GOSPEL

Matthew 28:16–20 "Go and make disciples of all nations."

(*Stand*)

P: This is the Gospel of the Lord.

C: PRAISE TO YOU, O CHRIST.

(*Be seated*)

THE CHILDREN'S SERMON

HYMN: "IN THE HOUR OF TRIAL" (*Lutheran Worship*, 511)

THE SERMON

The Letter to Philadelphia: Neglect—Locked Out in Death's Night

(*Stand*)

THE APOSTLES' CREED

(*Be seated*)

THE OFFERING

(*Stand*)

THE PRAYER OF THE DAY

ALL: Jesus, Son of David, Son of God, King of Your church, help me not only to endure suffering in faith but also to use the door You have opened to invite others to trust You. Give to me and all believers the crown of life that You have won for us. In Your saving name I pray. Amen.

THE PASTORAL PRAYERS

P: Lord, in Your mercy

C: HEAR OUR PRAYER.

THE LORD'S PRAYER

THE BENEDICTION

P: I am coming soon. Hold on to what you have, so that no one will take your crown. (Revelation 3:11)

C: HIM WHO OVERCOMES I WILL MAKE A PILLAR IN THE TEMPLE OF MY GOD. . . . AND I WILL ALSO WRITE ON HIM MY NEW NAME. (Revelation 3:12)

P: The grace of the Lord Jesus be with God's people. In the name of the Father and of the + Son and of the Holy Spirit.
C: AMEN.

CLOSING HYMN: "GUIDE ME EVER, GREAT REDEEMER" (*Lutheran Worship*, 220)

MAUNDY THURSDAY

COMPLACENCY—DEATH BY INDIFFERENCE

(*Stand*)

THE INVOCATION

P: In the name of the Father and of the + Son and of the Holy Spirit.

C: AMEN.

HYMN: "AWAKE, THOU SPIRIT OF THE WATCHMEN"
(*Lutheran Worship*, 315, stanza 1)

PSALM 106:1–6, 47–48

P: Praise the LORD. Give thanks to the LORD, for He is good; His love endures forever.

C: WHO CAN PROCLAIM THE MIGHTY ACTS OF THE LORD OR FULLY DECLARE HIS PRAISE?

P: Blessed are they who maintain justice, who constantly do what is right.

C: REMEMBER ME, O LORD, WHEN YOU SHOW FAVOR TO YOUR PEOPLE, COME TO MY AID WHEN YOU SAVE THEM,

P: That I may enjoy the prosperity of Your chosen ones, that I may share in the joy of Your nation and join Your inheritance in giving praise.

C: WE HAVE SINNED, EVEN AS OUR FATHERS DID; WE HAVE DONE WRONG AND ACTED WICKEDLY.

P: Save us, O LORD our God, and gather us from the nations, that we may give thanks to Your holy name and glory in Your praise.

ALL: Praise be to the LORD, the God of Israel, from everlasting to everlasting. Let all the people say, "Amen!" Praise the LORD.

HYMN: "AWAKE, THOU SPIRIT OF THE WATCHMEN"
(*Lutheran Worship*, 315, stanzas 2–3)

CONFESSION AND ABSOLUTION (*Hymnal Supplement 98*, p. 6)
(*Be seated*)

The First Lesson

Amos 6:1–7 "Woe to you who are complacent in Zion."

L: This is the Word of the Lord.

C: THANKS BE TO GOD.

The Epistle Lesson

Revelation 3:14–22 "I know your deeds, that you are neither cold nor hot."

L: This is the Word of the Lord.

C: THANKS BE TO GOD.

The Holy Gospel

Matthew 19:16–26 "Sell your possessions and give to the poor."

(*Stand*)

P: This is the Gospel of the Lord.

C: PRAISE TO YOU, O CHRIST.

(*Be seated*)

The Children's Sermon

Hymn: "Let Us Ever Walk with Jesus" (*Lutheran Worship*, 381)

(*Stand for the final stanza*)

The Sermon

The Letter to Laodicea: Complacency—Death by Indifference

(*Stand*)

The Nicene Creed

(*Be seated*)

The Offering

(*Stand*)

The Prayer of the Day

ALL: Dear Lord Jesus, the Amen, the faithful and true witness, the ruler of creation, ignite in my heart the fire of Your love that I might flee from all things hurtful and run to You. Cover my sin and shame and heal my eyes so I may see Your love for me. In Your name I pray. Amen.

The Pastoral Prayers

P: Lord, in Your mercy

C: HEAR OUR PRAYER.

THE LORD'S PRAYER

THE SERVICE OF HOLY COMMUNION

(*Be seated for Communion distribution*)

DISTRIBUTION HYMNS

"Jesus, Refuge of the Weary" (*Lutheran Worship*, 90)
"When I Survey the Wondrous Cross" (*Lutheran Worship*, 115)

THE STRIPPING OF THE ALTAR

(*Psalm 22 is chanted during the stripping of the altar. All leave in silence.*)

NOTES ON TENEBRAE SERVICE FOR WORSHIP LEADERS

Worshipers are instructed to enter the service in silence and leave in silence. There is no prelude or postlude. The altar and chancel should be stripped of all decorations, though a wall-mounted cross may be draped in black or a crucifix may be displayed.

The pastor may wear a cassock or an alb with no stole or cross. He also may wear black clergy attire. The acolyte and crucifer may wear an alb or black cassock.

Lights should be dimmed throughout the service. No offering should be taken. (A small table with the appropriate symbols of Christ's suffering may be placed at the entrance to the nave to hold an offering plate.) Hymns or choir selections may be included according to local custom. It is suggested that words to hymns be printed in the service folder.

The six candles that are extinguished during the recitation of the words from the cross may be placed in a row on the altar. The number of candles may be doubled and two candles may be extinguished after each of the six words. The seventh candle is the Christ or paschal candle. It is carried out of the chancel after the reading of the seventh word. It returns to the chancel still burning in hopeful anticipation of the resurrection.

There is no provision for Holy Communion in this service because it seems not to have been celebrated in the ancient church on Good Friday. All is done in a manner that contrasts sharply with the light and joy of Christ's resurrection on Easter Sunday.

A TENEBRAE SERVICE FOR GOOD FRIDAY

Seven Words for Seven Churches

The Processional of the Cross

(*Stand as the cross and Christ candle enter.*)

The Invocation

P: In the name of the Father and of the + Son and of the Holy Spirit.

C: AMEN.

Psalm 2 (Antiphon, Psalm 2:11–12b)

P: Serve the Lord with fear and rejoice with trembling.

C: BLESSED ARE ALL WHO TAKE REFUGE IN HIM.

P: Why do the nations conspire and the peoples plot in vain?

C: THE KINGS OF THE EARTH TAKE THEIR STAND AND THE RULERS GATHER TOGETHER AGAINST THE LORD AND AGAINST HIS ANOINTED ONE.

P: "Let us break their chains," they say, "and throw off their fetters."

C: THE ONE ENTHRONED IN HEAVEN LAUGHS; THE LORD SCOFFS AT THEM.

P: Then He rebukes them in His anger and terrifies them in His wrath, saying,

C: "I HAVE INSTALLED MY KING ON ZION, MY HOLY HILL."

P: I will proclaim the decree of the Lord: He said to me, "You are My Son; today I have become Your Father.

C: ASK OF ME, AND I WILL MAKE THE NATIONS YOUR INHERI-TANCE, THE ENDS OF THE EARTH YOUR POSSESSION.

P: You will rule them with an iron scepter; You will dash them to pieces like pottery."

C: THEREFORE, YOU KINGS, BE WISE; BE WARNED, YOU RULERS OF THE EARTH.

P: Serve the Lord with fear and rejoice with trembling.

C: KISS THE SON, LEST HE BE ANGRY AND YOU BE DESTROYED IN YOUR WAY, FOR HIS WRATH CAN FLARE UP IN A MOMENT. BLESSED ARE ALL WHO TAKE REFUGE IN HIM.

P: Serve the LORD with fear and rejoice with trembling.

C: BLESSED ARE ALL WHO TAKE REFUGE IN HIM.

CONFESSION AND ABSOLUTION (adapted from Revelation 2–3)

P: Let us confess our sins to our holy and gracious God.

(*Silence for personal reflection and prayer.*)

C: LORD, I CONFESS THAT AT TIMES I HAVE FORSAKEN YOU, MY FIRST LOVE. I HAVE TOLERATED FALSE TEACHING AND THE IMMORAL BEHAVIOR THAT GOES ALONG WITH IT. I WANT OTH-ERS TO THINK OF ME AS BEING ALIVE, BUT OFTEN MY FAITH SEEMS DEAD. MY DEEDS ARE NOT COMPLETE IN YOUR SIGHT, O GOD. I AM NEITHER COLD NOR HOT BUT LUKEWARM, DESERV-ING OF BEING SPIT OUT OF YOUR MOUTH. I THINK I AM RICH, THAT I HAVE ACQUIRED WEALTH AND NEED NOTHING. I DO NOT REALIZE THAT I AM WRETCHED, PITIFUL, POOR, BLIND, AND NAKED. I AM WORTHY ONLY OF YOUR REBUKE AND DISCI-PLINE, O LORD. GRANT ME AN EARNEST AND REPENTANT HEART. OPEN THE DOOR OF MY HEART TO YOU SO I MAY HEAR YOUR VOICE OF FORGIVENESS.

P: Our Lord Jesus Christ says, "To him who overcomes, I will give the right to sit with Me on My throne, just as I overcame and sat down with My Father on His throne" and "I will never blot out his name from the book of life, but will acknowledge his name before My Father and His angels." At the cross Jesus paid for all your sins, dying in your place. When He rose from the tomb, He defeated the power of sin, death, and the devil in your life. You have been baptized into the death, burial, and resurrec-tion of Christ and have humbly confessed your sins. Therefore, I, as a called minister of Christ, do at His command and in His stead forgive you all your sins in the name of the Father and of the + Son and of the Holy Spirit.

C: AMEN. THANKS BE TO GOD!

THE KYRIE

THE COLLECT

P: Let us pray. Gracious God in heaven, on this day Your blessed Son, Jesus Christ, endured unimaginable torment as He experienced abandonment by His friends, humiliation and torture from His enemies, and the despair of being forsaken by You, His Father. All this He suffered willingly that we might be graciously spared the penalty our sins deserve. As we meditate on His agony, move our hearts to repentance, faith, and thanksgiving that overflows in greater devotion to Him and love for others so You might be ever glorified in our lives. This we pray in Your name, eternally one God with the Son and the Holy Spirit.

C: AMEN.

(*Be seated*)

HYMN: "THE LAMB" (*Hymnal Supplement 98*, 822)

THE FIRST WORD: LUKE 23:34

"Father, forgive them, for they do not know what they are doing."

HYMN: "FROM CALVARY'S CROSS I HEARD CHRIST SAY"
(*Lutheran Worship*, 108, stanza 1)

THE SECOND WORD: LUKE 23:43

"I tell you the truth, today you will be with Me in paradise."

HYMN: "FROM CALVARY'S CROSS I HEARD CHRIST SAY"
(*Lutheran Worship*, 108, stanza 2)

THE THIRD WORD: JOHN 19:26B

"Dear woman, here is your son. . . . Here is your mother."

HYMN: "FROM CALVARY'S CROSS I HEARD CHRIST SAY"
(*Lutheran Worship*, 108, stanza 3)

THE FOURTH WORD: JOHN 19:28

"I am thirsty."

HYMN: "FROM CALVARY'S CROSS I HEARD CHRIST SAY"
(*Lutheran Worship*, 108, stanza 4)

THE FIFTH WORD: MATTHEW 27:46
"My God, My God, why have You forsaken Me?"

HYMN: "FROM CALVARY'S CROSS I HEARD CHRIST SAY"
(*Lutheran Worship*, 108, stanza 5)

THE SIXTH WORD: JOHN 19:28
"It is finished."

HYMN: "FROM CALVARY'S CROSS I HEARD CHRIST SAY"
(*Lutheran Worship*, 108, stanza 6)

THE SEVENTH WORD: LUKE 23:46
"Father, into Your hands I commit My spirit."

HYMN: "FROM CALVARY'S CROSS I HEARD CHRIST SAY"
(*Lutheran Worship*, 108, stanzas 7–8)

P: These are the words of Him who is the First and the Last, who died and came to life again. (Revelation 2:8)

C: HE WHO HAS AN EAR, LET HIM HEAR WHAT THE SPIRIT SAYS TO THE CHURCHES. (Revelation 2:7)

P: If anyone hears My voice and opens the door, I will come in and eat with him and he with Me. (Revelation 3:20)

C: HE WHO HAS AN EAR LET HIM HEAR WHAT THE SPIRIT SAYS TO THE CHURCHES. (Revelation 2:7)

HYMN: "JESUS, REMEMBER ME" (*Hymnal Supplement 98*, 827)

THE LORD'S PRAYER

SILENT RECESSIONAL

(*Face the cross as it exits.*)

A TENEBRAE SERVICE FOR GOOD FRIDAY

SEVEN WORDS FOR SEVEN CHURCHES

Reader's and Preacher's Copy
for the Words from the Cross

INTRODUCTION

Pastor: Since at least the fourth century, Christians have remembered the crucifixion of our Lord Jesus on Good Friday with special services and acts of devotion. The specifics have changed over the years, but generally the account of Jesus' suffering and death is retold with special attention given to His final seven words from the cross. We will do the same tonight, but we also will relate our Savior's passion to the experience of Christians who lived a half-century after Christ, as well as those who live twenty centuries after Christ.

Those of us who have lost loved ones know what is to cling to the memories of our last moments with them. We recite over and over any words they spoke. The Gospels also recount the last days and hours of Jesus. As much as one half of each Gospel is devoted to the events of Holy Week, though Jesus' earthly ministry lasted at least three years. Of those Gospel sections devoted to Jesus' passion, a considerable portion is devoted to the events of Good Friday. Whole chapters focus on the details of the crucifixion and the statements made by Jesus and others.

Such attention to one event tells us that Jesus' chief concern was not prophesying, teaching, healing, or performing miracles, though many of His prophecies, sermons, and miracles are recorded in Scripture. No, the most important thing Jesus did was die in the place of sinners. Thus on Good Friday, as has been done for centuries, we remember the manner in which Jesus died and the intimate thoughts He shared with us through His final seven words. These words have assured generations of repentant sinners that they are redeemed.

THE FIRST WORD

"Father, forgive them, for they do not know what they are doing." (Luke 23:34)

Pastor: It is unfortunate that fervency in religion and love for Christ are not the same. The church at Ephesus did good work and defended the faith against heresy, but Jesus was far from the center of its life. Through the angel, Jesus said to the Ephesian Christians, "You have forsaken your first love" (Revelation 2:4). How many of us today pose as champions of orthodoxy but speak contemptuously of another whose faith we consider suspect? Likewise, it was a religious crowd that gathered at the foot of the cross to ridicule and torment Jesus. These people knew Scripture and fancied themselves to be the covenant children of God, yet their words and behavior revealed hearts far from God.

Like the Ephesian Christians and the Jews, we often forsake our first love. But Jesus never forsook His first love. Jesus loved us when we didn't love Him. His first love drove Him to the cross to give His life as a sacrifice for our sins. He even prayed, "Father forgive them for they do not know what they are doing" (Luke 23:34). Through faith in Christ, we are grafted into the family of God, embraced by His divine love. Hear now the hate-filled words of sinners against Christ and His words of love spoken to God for them.

Reader 1: "You who are going to destroy the temple and build it in three days, save Yourself!" (Matthew 27:40).

Reader 2: "If You are the King of the Jews, save Yourself" (Luke 23:37).

Reader 1: "He saved others, but He can't save Himself" (Mark 15:31).

Reader 2: "He's the King of Israel! Let him come down now from the cross, and we will believe in Him" (Matthew 27:42).

Reader 1: "He trusts in God. Let God rescue Him now if He wants Him, for He said, 'I am the Son of God'" (Matthew 27:43).

Pastor: Besides the religious leaders and the people in the crowd, the soldiers and even the two condemned criminals joined in the verbal abuse of Jesus. One of the criminals, nailed to a cross beside Jesus, shouted out:

Reader 2: "Aren't You the Christ? Save Yourself and us!" (Luke 23:39).

Pastor: But no hateful reply came from Jesus' lips. Instead, He said:

Reader 1: "Father, forgive them, for they do not know what they are doing." (Luke 23:34).

(*The first candle is extinguished. The bell sounds. The first stanza of* Lutheran Worship, *108, is sung.*)

THE SECOND WORD

"I tell you the truth, today you will be with Me in paradise." (Luke 23:43)

Pastor: Jesus said to the persecuted church in Smyrna, "Be faithful even to the point of death and I will give you the crown of life" (Revelation 2:10). How many of us received these words as a confirmation verse? When we heard these words as our own on that special day, we believed them with all our heart. Our faith was firm and clear. We promised to willingly suffer all, even death, rather than fall away from Christ and His church. Then we got a driver's license, a job, a girlfriend or a boyfriend, and the words faded from our memory. We hadn't suffered a thing and already we were Christians in name only.

Although we are often forgetful of promises we make to God, He does not forget His promises to us. Our status as children of God, the forgiveness of sins, the gift of righteousness and eternal life remain our greatest treasures because Jesus was faithful to the point of death in our place. Again and again on Good Friday, Jesus endured scorn and persecution to give us the crown of life.

In times of persecution, disaster, plague, famine, and war, the presence and fear of death is magnified. The persecuted church at Smyrna—faced with slander, prison, and martyrdom—was assured by Jesus: "He who overcomes will not be hurt at all by the second death" (Revelation 2:11). But how does one overcome? By faith, by trusting Jesus. This is demonstrated by Jesus' word to a dying thief. Even on the cross, Jesus had overcome the world, sin, death, and the devil. Those who by faith are in Christ have also overcome. Such was the case of the thief on the cross who confessed his faith in Jesus.

Reader 2: One of the criminals who hung there hurled insults at Him: "Aren't You the Christ? Save Yourself and us!" But the other criminal rebuked him. "Don't you fear God," he said, "since you are under the same sentence? We are punished justly, for we are getting what our deeds deserve. But this man has done nothing wrong." Then he said, "Jesus, remember me when You come into Your kingdom." Jesus answered him,

Reader 1: "I tell you the truth, today you will be with Me in paradise" (Luke 23:39–43).

(The second candle is extinguished. The bell sounds. The second stanza of Lutheran Worship, *108, is sung.)*

THE THIRD WORD

"Dear woman, here is your son. . . . Here is your mother." (John 19:26–27)
Pastor: To the church at Pergamum, Jesus said, "These are the words of Him who has the sharp, double-edged sword" (Revelation 2:12). That sword is the Word of God, and what a powerful sword it is! An offensive weapon, God's Word strikes at our hearts, stripping away all our defenses, exposing our sin and guilt. Then, amazingly, when we stand condemned as sinners, the same Word defends us from the punishment we deserve. "Neither do I condemn you," Jesus said to the adulteress and to you and me. "Go now and leave your life of sin" (John 8:11). We come to the cross, driven by God's sword of law, guilty, quivering, and ashamed. We leave, defended by His sword of grace, forgiven, righteous, and redeemed. An angel guarded the entrance to the Garden of Eden with a fiery sword to keep people out, but Christ with His sword welcomes us in to paradise.

When Jesus was circumcised, Simeon said to Mary, "A sword will pierce your own soul" (Luke 2:35). This happened when Mary witnessed the suffering and death of her child. It was the sword of pain, the sword of Christian suffering and affliction. Yet when Christ sends the cross into your life, He also sends the consolation of the Holy Spirit so we might be conformed to His image. As Jesus said to the church at Pergamum, who overcame through the means of grace, "I will give some of the hidden manna" that leads to everlasting life (Revelation 2:17). Jesus is the bread of life, imparting Himself in the Sacrament of the Altar. He provides bread for our souls. But in this third word from the cross, we see Jesus, the human son, providing for the material needs of His mother. And He cares for all of us in the same manner.
Reader 2: Near the cross of Jesus stood His mother, His mother's sister, Mary the wife of Clopas, and Mary Magdalene. When Jesus saw His mother there, and the disciple whom He loved standing nearby, He said to His mother,
Reader 1: "Dear woman, here is your son,"
Reader 2: and to the disciple,
Reader 1: "Here is your mother."
Reader 2: From that time on, this disciple took her into his home. (John 19:25–27)

(The third candle is extinguished. The bell sounds. The third stanza of Lutheran Worship, 108, is sung.)

THE FOURTH WORD

"I am thirsty." (John 19:28)

Pastor: To the church at Thyatira, Jesus said, "These are the words of the Son of God, whose eyes are like blazing fire and whose feet are like burnished bronze" (Revelation 2:18). Is this the same Jesus whose suffering we read of in the Gospels? In His trials we see Jesus stripped, beaten, mocked, and crucified. In His agony He whispers, "I am thirsty" (John 19:28). Yes, this is the same Jesus. It is the human, mortal, and vulnerable Jesus, the Jesus of humiliation. This Jesus allows Himself to endure unspeakable torment, not because He is weak and helpless—He could have called ten legions of angels to His side—but because He is strong to save, strong to keep His face set toward Jerusalem and the cross so He might help the helpless, you and me.

After His atoning death, Jesus Christ rose from the dead in glory. Someday, we will see the Christ of glory—the Jesus whose eyes are like blazing fire and feet like burnished bronze. This is how we will see Jesus when He comes again at the Last Day. He will come with an eternal reward for you, His faithful servants.

What a dramatic contrast we see between the Jesus who comes as judge of the nations on the Last Day and the Jesus who dies on the cross at Calvary. Those who persevere in faith despite pervasive evil are promised "authority over the nations" (Revelation 2:26). The unrepentant nations on the day of Christ's return will be ruled by Him with an iron scepter and dashed to pieces like pottery. But the Jesus who dies can scarcely lift His head to wet His swollen and dry lips with the cheap wine raised up to Him on a hyssop branch. "Blessed are those who hunger and thirst for righteousness, for they will be filled" (Matthew 5:6). Christ is your righteousness, and He quenches your thirst with the water of life.

Reader 2: Later, knowing that all was now completed, and so that the Scripture would be fulfilled, Jesus said,

Reader 1: "I am thirsty."

Reader 2: A jar of wine vinegar was there, so they soaked a sponge in it, put the sponge on a stalk of the hyssop plant, and lifted it to Jesus' lips. (John 19:28–29)

(The fourth candle is extinguished. The bell sounds. The fourth stanza of Lutheran Worship, *108, is sung.)*

The Fifth Word

"My God, My God, why have You forsaken Me?" (Matthew 27:46)

Pastor: To the church at Sardis, Jesus wrote, "I know your deeds" (Revelation 3:1). These are words that apply to each person involved in the crucifixion drama. Some at the trial shout: "Let His blood be on us and on our children" (Matthew 27:25). Jesus hears such words and the irony in them, a curse and yet a plea for salvation. He notes the words of those who sneer with bitter sarcasm, "He's the King of Israel! Let Him come down now from the cross" (Matthew 27:42). Jesus looks into the heart of the centurion who efficiently does his job even as he begins to believe that Jesus is the Son of God. Jesus gazes intently into the locked room in which the disciples hide, frightened and ashamed. They had forsaken Him, friends and enemies alike. Even His Father had forsaken Him. But this was for the purpose of redemption. Jesus endured the curse of God for you and me so we might receive the blessing of God.

As Jesus looks, His gaze is not vindictive. It is one of pity. It is a gaze of sadness for those who would spurn his love and grace. It is a look of welcome and forgiveness to those who take unsteady steps of faith and return to His open arms. "I know your deeds," says Jesus, "even better than you know them yourselves. They are not complete. They fall far short of the demands of God's Law. But I can make you and your deeds whole and perfect."

Being a member of a struggling and persecuted minority affects people in different ways. Consider the church at Sardis. Most members seemed to keep quiet about their faith, trying to find acceptance and avoid trouble. Jail, torture, and death were real possibilities in first-century Sardis and remain so in some parts of the world today. How reassuring it is for suffering Christians to hear Jesus say, "I will never blot out (your) name from the book of life" (Revelation 3:5). The cross tells us that God is not punishing us; instead, Jesus took the punishment we deserved.

Reader 2: From the sixth hour until the ninth hour darkness came over all the land. About the ninth hour Jesus cried out in a loud voice,

Reader 1: "*Eloi, Eloi, lama sabachthani?*"—which means "My God, My God, why have You forsaken Me?"

Reader 2: When some of those standing there heard this, they said, "He's calling Elijah." (Matthew 27:45–46)
(*The fifth candle is extinguished. The bell sounds. The fifth stanza of* Lutheran Worship, *108, is sung.*)

THE SIXTH WORD

"It is finished!" (John 19:28)

Pastor: To the church at Philadelphia, Jesus said, "I will also keep you from the hour of trial" (Revelation 3:10). You might find it puzzling that Jesus could keep a congregation—or you and me—from the hour of trial but not Himself. That was, of course, one of the taunts hurled at Jesus as He hung from the cross: "He saved others but He can't save Himself" (Matthew 27:42). Actually, it isn't that Jesus couldn't save Himself. It is that He, in perfect agreement with His heavenly Father, had chosen not to save Himself so He could save us. This was the divine plan. Because of sin, man brought on himself suffering, death, and eternal banishment from God. But in love God could not leave man to his hopelessness. The Father would send the Son to be the sin-bearer for the whole human race.

Jesus willingly undertook this role, being born a helpless baby, living the holy life we had neglected, facing temptation and defeating it where we had failed, enduring the humiliation of false accusations and mockery, submitting to torture and death on a cross. On that cross Jesus finished His work, fully and completely winning salvation for all people.

Christians will face the rage of unbelieving enemies, suffering, and death. But those enemies ultimately will not win. We have the guarantee of Christ's resurrection on Easter morning and the seal of Holy Baptism, the most precious possession of the believer. Baptized into Jesus Christ's death, burial, and resurrection, every evil becomes temporary and limited.

The church at Philadelphia was a congregation that held fast to its faith without compromise. Jesus promised: "Him who overcomes I will make a pillar in the house of My God" (Revelation 3:12). One day the struggle would be over, and the saints in Philadelphia could go home. Jesus makes His promise to us as well. It is a promise that will be kept not because of our faithfulness in doing the work God has given us but because of Jesus' faithfulness to do the work God gave Him. At Calvary, Jesus' work of saving you and me was finished.

Reader 2: When He had received the drink, Jesus said,

Reader 1: "It is finished."

Reader 2: With that, He bowed His head and gave up His spirit. (John 19:30)

(*The sixth candle is extinguished. The bell sounds. The sixth stanza of* Lutheran Worship, *108, is sung.*)

THE SEVENTH WORD

"Father, into Your hands I commit My spirit!" (Luke 23:46)

Pastor: To the church at Laodicea, Jesus said, "I counsel you to buy from Me gold refined in the fire, so you can become rich; and white clothes to wear, so you can cover your shameful nakedness." We are supposed to buy gold, riches, and clothes from Jesus? Wasn't Jesus poor and homeless? The riches and white garments Jesus offers are not something one can buy in a store. The Christians of Laodicea, like you and me, had full purses and stuffed closets. They were materialistic. They committed their spirits not to God but to the things of this world. With no hope of heaven, however, riches mean absolutely nothing.

The riches Jesus offers are the blessings of salvation He obtains for us through His suffering and death. A great exchange takes place at the cross. There Jesus takes our filthy rags of sin, our debt to God and neighbor, the burden of guilt and the wrath of God we have incurred and places them all on Himself. Then in our Baptism, Jesus clothes us with the dazzling white garments of His righteousness, declaring us to be the children of God and heirs of heaven.

To all who trust in Him, Jesus says, "I will give the right to sit with Me on My throne, just as I overcame and sat down with My Father on His throne" (Revelation 3:21). In His final statement from the cross, we see the moment of triumph as Jesus overcomes sin and Satan and entrusts Himself to His Father. At the moment of your death, Jesus will commit your spirit into the sure and loving hands of your merciful heavenly Father.

Reader 2: It was now about the sixth hour, and darkness came over the whole land until the ninth hour, for the sun stopped shining. And the curtain of the temple was torn in two. Jesus called out with a loud voice,

Reader 1: "Father, into Your hands I commit My spirit." (Luke 23:44–46)

(*The Christ candle is carried out of the chancel, still burning. Seven bells sound. The seventh and eighth stanzas of* Lutheran Worship, *108, are sung.*)

CONCLUSION

Reader 2: When He had said this, He breathed His last. The centurion, seeing what had happened, praised God and said, "Surely this was a righteous man." When all the people who had gathered to witness this sight saw what took place, they beat their breasts and went away. But all those who knew Him, including the women who had followed Him from Galilee, stood at a distance, watching these things. (Luke 23:46–49)

Pastor: Our narrative draws rapidly to its conclusion. Jesus is dead. A soldier pierced His side with a spear to make sure. Just before sunset, Pilate released the body of Jesus to Joseph of Arimathea and the women watched as Jesus was hastily buried in a borrowed tomb. They made plans to finish preparing His body for burial on Sunday morning. A heavy stone was rolled into place to seal the tomb.

(*Loudly close a large book to symbolize the closing of the tomb. Conclude with the order of service as included previously.*)

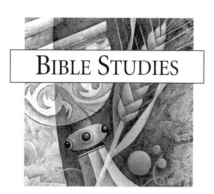

BIBLE STUDIES

LETTER TO THE FIRST ANGEL

WORDS OF LIFE FOR EPHESUS AND ME

Revelation 2:1–7

THEME VERSE

"Yet I hold this against you: You have forsaken your first love."
Revelation 2:4

OPENING UP

1. What values did you learn from your parents that still guide you today?

2. What is one of the most important goals you have reached so far? How did you overcome the obstacles?

SETTING THE STAGE

- the Son of Man
- *angel* means
- John and Patmos
- the city of Ephesus
- Paul and Ephesus
- Nestorianism
- the number seven
- the Nicolaitans

DIGGING IN

1. What are the "seven stars" and the "seven lampstands?" See John's explanation in 1:20. Who is the one who "holds" the stars and "walks" among the lampstands? See 1:13.

2. Locate and list the seven reasons Jesus commends the church at Ephesus. See 2:2–3 and 2:6.

3. What does Jesus hold against the Ephesians? See 2:4. Jesus implies that doing good and maintaining right doctrine aren't enough. What's essential? See 1:5.

4. How can one who possesses such fine characteristics as those listed in 2:2–3 be "fallen"? See Ephesians 2:8–9; Isaiah 14:12–15; Galatians 1:9; and Galatians 3:11.

5. What will happen to a church, such as the one at Ephesus, that loses its first love and does not repent? See 2:5. Note: "Repent" means to change one's mind and direction. It means to turn from sin to Christ and the righteousness that is by faith. From which sins do the Ephesians need to repent?

6. Jesus hates something in 2:6. What is it?

7. If the Nicolaitans are compared to Balaam and Balak, what must their beliefs and practices have included? See 2:14 and Numbers 23:7–12; 24:1–11; 25:1–3.

8. What sort of "ear" hears the message of the Spirit to the churches? See 2:7 and Romans 12:17.

9. What promise does Jesus make to those who overcome, that is, to those who repent and return to Christ, their first love? See 2:7.

THINK ABOUT IT

1. We began by noting that Jesus walks among the seven lampstands and holds the seven stars. What comfort and encouragement does this knowledge hold for the Ephesians and for us?

2. How has your love for Christ grown cold? In view of 2:7, how will Christ restore your love?

3. Do we "eat of the tree of life" (2:7) by partaking of the Lord's Supper? How is this a foretaste of paradise?

PRAYER

Jesus, Son of Man and Lord of the church, help me compare myself to the standards in Your Word and see where I have fallen short. Forgive me for my sins and give me a love for You that places You first in my life. Move me daily to share Your saving love with my neighbor. In Your name I pray. Amen.

LETTER TO THE FIRST ANGEL

WORDS OF LIFE FOR EPHESUS AND ME

Revelation 2:1–7

(Leader)

THEME VERSE

"Yet I hold this against you: You have forsaken your first love."
Revelation 2:4

OPENING UP

1. What values did you learn from your parents that still guide you today?

2. What is one of the most important goals you have reached so far? How did you overcome the obstacles?

SETTING THE STAGE

- In 1:12–16, one like a "son of man" appears to John while "in the Spirit" on the Lord's Day, that is, Sunday. In Daniel 7:13–14, the son of man is a messianic figure. John wants his readers to understand that the son of man in his vision is the same son of man as in Daniel's vision. Clearly, the resurrected, glorified Jesus is the Son of Man. Jesus gives John letters for the "angels" of the seven churches in Asia, the western part of modern day Turkey.

- "Angel" simply means "messenger," and it can refer to a spiritual being created by God to serve His people or to a pastor who brings God's message to the congregation. Because angels in the spiritual sense are so prominent in Revelation, this is probably the meaning John intends.

- John, an elderly prisoner on the Island of Patmos (1:9) in the Aegean Sea just off the coast of Asia, is directed to send the first letter to the angel of the church at Ephesus (1:19; 2:1).

- Ephesus is the nearest city in a clockwise circuit of seven cities in Asia. It was a provincial capital, a port city, and the site of one of the seven wonders of the ancient world, the Temple of Artemis, whose image supposedly fell from the sky. Perhaps her image was crafted from a meteorite.

- Paul labored in Ephesus and started the church there. A riot took place when silversmiths, who made idols of Artemis, began losing business because of the growing influence of Christianity. See Acts 19:23–41.

- In A.D. 431, the Third General Council of the Church met at Ephesus and condemned Nestorianism. Nestorianism was the false doctrine "that there were two separate Persons in the Incarnate Christ, the one Divine and the other Human, as opposed to the orthodox doctrine that the Incarnate Christ was a single Person, at once God and man" (*Oxford Dictionary of the Christian Church* [1957], p. 946).

- The prominence of the number seven is obvious in Revelation and in the letter to the church at Ephesus. Seven is the number of completion, perfection, or wholeness.

- The Nicolaitans are mentioned here and in the letter to the church at Pergamum (2:15). According to later tradition, this group followed Nicolas, the deacon of the early church (see Acts 6:5) who allegedly became a false teacher. But there is no early evidence to support this.

DIGGING IN

1. What are the "seven stars" and the "seven lampstands?" See John's explanation in 1:20. *"The seven stars are the angels of the seven churches, and the seven lampstands are the seven churches."* Who is the one who "holds" the stars and "walks" among the lampstands? See 1:13. *He is "someone like a son of man," that is, Christ.*

2. Locate and list the seven reasons Jesus commends the church at Ephesus. See 2:2–3 and 2:6. *(1) deeds (2) hard work (3) perseverance (4) cannot tolerate wicked men (5) have tested those who claim to be apostles but are not and have found them false (6) endured hardships for His name and have not grown weary (7) hate the practices of the Nicolaitans.*

3. What does Jesus hold against the Ephesians? See 2:4. *"You have forsaken your first love."* Jesus implies that doing good and maintaining right doc-

trine are not enough. What is essential? See 1:5. *The essential thing is knowing by faith "Him who loves us and has freed us from our sins by His blood," that is, Jesus. Good deeds and right doctrine are worthless apart from being justified by faith in Christ, our first love.*

4. How can one who possesses such fine characteristics as those listed in 2:2–3 be "fallen"? See Ephesians 2:8–9; Isaiah 14:12–15; Galatians 1:9; and Galatians 3:11. *One characterized only by good deeds and orthodoxy has exchanged justification by grace through faith for justification by good works or legalism. This places one in the same fallen category as Lucifer and results in condemnation.*

5. What will happen to a church, such as the one at Ephesus, that loses its first love and does not repent? See 2:5. *"I will come to you and remove your lampstand from its place."* Note: "Repent" means to change one's mind and direction. It means to turn from sin to Christ and the righteousness that is by faith. From which sins do the Ephesians need to repent? *They should turn from any form of sin or self-righteousness and trust only in Christ and His righteousness.*

6. Jesus hates something in 2:6. What is it? *He hates the practices of the Nicolaitans.*

7. If the Nicolaitans are compared to Balaam and Balak, what must their beliefs and practices have included? See 2:14 and Numbers 23:7–12; 24:1–11; 25:1–3. *Mixture of true and false doctrine, and the practice of sexual immorality are associated with Balaam, Balak, and Moab. Thus the Nicolaitans must have promoted a mixed Christian and pagan religion that advocated or tolerated sexual immorality.*

8. What sort of "ear" hears the message of the Spirit to the churches? See 2:7 and Romans 12:17. *A spiritual ear, an ear that hears with faith, hears the message of the Spirit.*

9. What promise does Jesus make to those who overcome, that is, to those who repent and return to Christ, their first love? See 2:7. *"I will give the right to eat from the tree of life, which is in the paradise of God."*

THINK ABOUT IT

1. We began by noting that Jesus walks among the seven lampstands and holds the seven stars. What comfort and encouragement does this

knowledge hold for the Ephesians and for us? *He is present to help and hold His people. He will not let them slip away. The call to repent comes from the loving heart of God and contains the power of His mercy.*

2. How has your love for Christ grown cold? In view of 2:7, how will Christ restore your love?

3. Do we "eat of the tree of life" (2:7) by partaking of the Lord's Supper? How is this a foretaste of paradise?

PRAYER

Jesus, Son of Man and Lord of the church, help me compare myself to the standards in Your Word and see where I have fallen short. Forgive me for my sins and give me a love for You that places You first in my life. Move me daily to share Your saving love with my neighbor. In Your name I pray. Amen.

LETTER TO THE SECOND ANGEL

WORDS OF LIFE FOR SMYRNA AND ME

Revelation 2:8–11

THEME VERSE

"I will give you the crown of life." Revelation 2:10

OPENING UP

1. When you were young, did you think of your family as poor or rich? Why?

2. If something frightens or worries you, who is the first person with whom you talk? What qualities does this person possess?

3. What is the most meaningful award you have ever received?

SETTING THE STAGE

- the city of Smyrna
- Christian difficulties and persecution
- Polycarp
- Uniqueness of this letter

DIGGING IN

1. What does the description "the First and the Last" proclaim about Christ? See 2:8. See also 1:8; 1:17; 21:6; 22:13; and Colossians 1:15–18.

2. Having established who Jesus Christ is, what two events does John single out as being the most important things Christ has done? See 2:8.

3. What two problems challenge the Christians in Smyrna? See 2:9. How might one problem have led to the other?

4. How does the death and resurrection of Jesus (2:8) make the Christians rich? See 2:9. See also Romans 8:31–39 and 1 Peter 1:4.

5. "Slander" in 2:9 is literally "blasphemy," which means "to throw an utterance" or an abusive, untrue accusation. Who is being blasphemed? What might be the substance of the blasphemy?

6. Those who are called "Jews and are not" are physically Jews but are not Jews spiritually. How can this be? See 2:9. See also Romans 4:7–17 and Galatians 3:26–29. "Satan" means "slanderer" or "accuser." Why would John call the assembly of Jews in Smyrna "a synagogue of Satan?" See John 8:44.

7. What prediction is made in 2:10? How long will the predicted event last? Is this a literal or symbolic number? Explain your answer.

8. What certainty awaits those who are "faithful, even to the point of death?" See 2:10. Note that the Greek word *stephanos* is translated here as "crown." This was a garland or wreath worn by victorious athletes, not a "diadem" worn by royalty. Why would "stephanos" be more appropriate? Although the crown of life is promised, is it something earned or is it a gift of faith? See 1:5b–6; 2:9a; Romans 1:17; Romans 10:9–10; and Ephesians 2:8–9.

9. What does it mean to hear "what the Spirit says to the churches? See 2:11. See also Romans 10:17.

10. What is "the second death" that will not hurt those who overcome? See 2:11. See also 20:6, 14.

Think about It

1. How does an awareness that Christ knows our "afflictions" and "poverty" bring comfort?

2. What false accusations do non-Christians make against Christ and the church today? How would you answer these accusations?

3. In times of suffering, some people abandon faith while others grow stronger. How might you explain these two outcomes?

4. What resources does God give to Christians to strengthen them in life's struggles? When was your faith strengthened?

PRAYER

Lord Jesus, You are the First and the Last, the one who died for my sins and came to life again. Help me know that Your Word is true no matter what others may say. Through Your Word give me courage to remain faithful in all life's struggles and to bear joyful witness to You. When my "ten days" are finished, grant me the crown of life You won for me that I might always be with You in heaven. In Your name I pray. Amen.

LETTER TO THE SECOND ANGEL

WORDS OF LIFE FOR SMYRNA AND ME

Revelation 2:8–11

(Leader)

THEME VERSE

"I will give you the crown of life." Revelation 2:10

OPENING UP

1. When you were young, did you think of your family as poor or rich? Why?

2. If something frightens or worries you, who is the first person with whom you talk? What qualities does that person possess?

3. What is the most meaningful award you have ever received?

SETTING THE STAGE

- Smyrna (modern Izmir, Turkey) is about 40 miles north of Ephesus in the circuit of the seven churches in Revelation. A wealthy and beautiful seaport with a library, stadium, theater, and temples, it was considered the "crown" of Asia. The word "crown" in 2:10 may relate to Smyrna's fame as a site for athletic games in which winners received garlands.

- Smyrna was destroyed in 580 B.C. and rebuilt in 290 B.C. according to a comprehensive plan. Perhaps John sees the city as an illustration of the resurrection.

- As an early and voluntary ally of Rome, Smyrna had temples to the goddess of Rome, the emperor Tiberius, and the Roman Senate.

- Christians in Smyrna faced the hostility of both pagans and members of a large Jewish community.

- Polycarp, bishop of Smyrna, was born about A.D. 69 and could have known the apostle John whose writing he quotes. A defender of orthodoxy, Polycarp was martyred about A.D.155 because he refused to deny his faith in Christ.

- Of the seven letters, only the letter to Smyrna contains no specific criticism or warning.

DIGGING IN

1. What does the description "the First and the Last" proclaim about Christ? See 2:8. See also 1:8, 17; 21:6; 22:13; and Colossians 1:15–18. *"Alpha and Omega" are the first and last letters of the Greek alphabet and are used to describe "the Lord God, who is, and who was, and who is to come, the Almighty" (Revelation 1:8). Jesus Christ is called "the First and the Last," who was dead and is alive for ever and ever. Because both "Alpha and Omega" and "First and Last" are used to describe the Lord God, the Almighty, and Christ, John is proclaiming the full deity of Jesus Christ. This is consistent with Paul's doctrine that Jesus Christ is the creator of all things and is before all things.*

2. Having established who Jesus Christ is, what two events does John single out as being the most important things Christ has done? See 2:8. *Christ died and came to life again.*

3. What two problems challenge the Christians in Smyrna? See 2:9. *Afflictions and poverty.* How might one problem have led to the other? *Persecution as members of an illegal religion no doubt meant the loss of property and livelihood. Thus many early Christians were extremely poor.*

4. How does the death and resurrection of Jesus (2:8) make Christians rich? See 2:9. See also Romans 8:31–39 and 1 Peter 1:4. *Christians are rich with the blessings of salvation. They have an inheritance in heaven that can never fade. They are justified and can never be separated from the love of God.*

5. "Slander" in 2:9 is literally "blasphemy," which means "to throw an utterance" or an abusive, untrue accusation. Who is being blasphemed? *Christ is being blasphemed as are, by association, those who believe in Him, that is, Christians.* What might be the substance of the blasphemy? *Some people deny that Jesus is the Son of God, the Messiah who died for sinners and rose from*

the dead. The Christians who do believe this are perhaps being accused of atheism because they adhere to neither paganism nor Judaism, the two legal religions. They are also perhaps being called traitors because they refuse to worship the emperor.

6. Those who are called "Jews and are not" are physically Jews but are not Jews spiritually. How can this be? See 2:9. See also Romans 4:7–17 and Galatians 3:26–29. *Being a true child of Abraham is not a matter of physical descent, law keeping, or circumcision but a matter of having the faith of Abraham. Possessing the faith of Abraham means receiving the gift of righteousness by faith in Abraham's descendant, Jesus. To reject Jesus is to deny Abraham's faith and thus not be a Jew at all.* "Satan" means "slanderer" or "accuser." Why would John call the assembly of Jews in Smyrna "a synagogue of Satan"? (2:9). See John 8:44. *The Jews in Smyrna are slandering the Christians and their faith in a particularly vicious way. Thus they are assisting Satan, showing themselves to be his children, not God's.*

7. What prediction is made in 2:10? *The Christians in Smyrna are about to suffer persecution.* How long will the predicted event last? *Ten days.* Is this a literal or symbolic number? *Symbolic.* Explain your answer. *"Ten days" implies a limited but nonetheless intense period of persecution.*

8. What certainty awaits those who are "faithful, even to the point of death?" See 2:10. *The crown of life.* Note that the Greek word *stephanos* is translated here as "crown." This was a garland or wreath worn by victorious athletes, not a "diadem" worn by royalty. Why would "stephanos" be more appropriate? *One is born into royalty, but the victor's crown awarded in an athletic game implies struggle and pain.* Although the crown of life is promised, is it something earned or is it a gift of faith? See 1:5b–6; 2:9a; Romans 1:17; Romans 10:9–10; and Ephesians 2:8–9. *Eternal life is a gift of faith.*

9. What does it mean to hear "what the Spirit says to the churches" (2:11)? See Romans 10:17. *To hear means to respond in faith to the word proclaimed. Those who hear the Spirit will remain faithful through persecution and receive the promise of life.*

10. What is "the second death" that will not hurt those who overcome? See 2:11. See also 20:6. *The second death is the lake of fire, into which Death and Hell are thrown.*

THINK ABOUT IT

1. How does an awareness that Christ knows our "afflictions" and "poverty" bring comfort?

2. What false accusations do non-Christians make against Christ and the church today? How would you answer these accusations?

3. In times of suffering, some people abandon faith while others grow stronger. How might you explain these two outcomes?

4. What resources does God give to Christians to strengthen them in life's struggles? When was your faith strengthened?

PRAYER

Lord Jesus, You are the First and the Last, the one who died for my sins and came to life again. Help me know that Your Word is true no matter what others may say. Through Your Word give me courage to remain faithful in all life's struggles and to bear joyful witness to You. When my "ten days" are finished, grant me the crown of life You won for me that I might always be with You in heaven. In Your name I pray. Amen.

LETTER TO THE THIRD ANGEL

WORDS OF LIFE FOR PERGAMUM AND ME

REVELATION 2:12–17

THEME VERSE

"I know where you live—where Satan has his throne. Yet you remain true
to My name." Revelation 2:12a

OPENING UP

1. What is your favorite place to eat? How did you find it?

2. How has a Christian relative or friend been a help or inspiration to
   you?

3. From whom are you most likely to take advice? Why?

SETTING THE STAGE

- the city of Pergamum
- religion in Pergamum
- Antipas

DIGGING IN

1. In what sense does Christ hold a double-edged sword? See 2:12. See
   also 1:16; Ephesians 6:17; and Hebrews 4:12. Is the double-edged sword
   Law that condemns or Gospel that saves?

2. In view of the information presented above, why does "where Satan's
   throne is" aptly describe Pergamum? See 2:13.

3. What price have the Pergamum Christians paid because they have
   remained true to Christ? See 2:13b. The word *witness* in Greek literally
   means "martyr." So many faithful witnesses for Jesus died in the early
   days of Christianity that to be a witness became synonymous with being

one who died for Jesus.

4. The Christians of Pergamum defended the faith at great personal cost, yet they were not without fault. What does John have against them? See 2:14–15. For the account of Balaam and Balak, see Numbers 22:1–25; 31:1–16. Scripture gives no further information on the origins or practices of the Nicolaitans. What does the letter to the Christians of Pergamum imply that the church should do about those who teach falsely?

5. How will repentance be evidenced? See 2:16. Who gives the church the right to judge doctrine and behavior? See Matthew 16:13–19; John 20:19–23; 1 Corinthians 5:1–5; 2 Corinthians 2:5–11; Galatians 1:6–9; and 2 John 7–11.

6. Meat sacrificed to idols was perhaps all that was available in some Gentile communities. Paul says eating it is alright in most cases. When is it harmful? See 1 Corinthians 8:4–13. What must have been happening at Pergamum to bring about the warning in 2:14?

7. What does Christ threaten if the Christians at Pergamum do not repent? How will Christ fulfill His threat? See 2:16.

8. Those who overcome, that is, those who repent and believe in Christ Jesus, are given two promises. What are they? See 2:17.

9. How can one know that he or she is receiving the "white stone"? See John 20:31 and Acts 2:38–39.

Think about It

1. What is the purpose of excommunication? Is it done to publicly retain the sins of unrepentant persons and bar them from Holy Communion, or is it intended to restore these individuals to fellowship through repentance and forgiveness?

2. Why is church discipline so seldom practiced these days?

3. What in our culture might be similar to the practices of Balaam and the Nicolaitans?

4. Christians are free to do those things the Word of God neither forbids nor mentions. When should a Christian voluntarily limit this freedom? When should Christians refuse to limit this freedom?

5. How does bearing the name of the triune God in Baptism affect one's daily life?

Prayer

Gracious Savior, You have delivered me from all my sins through faith in Your sure word of forgiveness. Help me be watchful against all things harmful to me and my brothers and sisters. Give me boldness to turn from sin and live my repentance daily. Thank You that in Baptism, the triune God has named me as His own. In Jesus' name I pray. Amen.

LETTER TO THE THIRD ANGEL

WORDS OF LIFE FOR PERGAMUM AND ME

Revelation 2:12–17

(Leader)

THEME VERSE

"I know where you live—where Satan has his throne. Yet you remain true to My name." Revelation 2:12a

OPENING UP

What is your favorite place to eat? How did you find it?

How has a Christian relative or friend been a help or inspiration to you?

From whom are you most likely to take advice? Why?

SETTING THE STAGE

- Pergamum is now Bergama, Turkey. It is located 50 miles north of Smyrna on a 1,000-foot high hill, 15 miles from the Aegean Sea. Pergamum was willed to Rome by its last king in 133 B.C.

- By the second century, Pergamum was a center of art, culture, and religion. Parchment was developed in this city as a substitute for papyrus. A great library held 200,000 parchment scrolls.

- A great altar to Zeus was located in Pergamum, as well as temples honoring Dionysus and Athena, the city's patron goddess. A temple to Asclepius the Greek god of healing, whose image was a serpent, made Pergamum the pagan equivalent of Lourdes. "Satan's throne" (2:13) may be a reference to the city's prominence as the chief center of the imperial cult in this part of the world (Pergamum featured three temples dedicated to the emperor), or it may refer to the generally over-whelming pagan character of the city.

• Antipas, the faithful martyr in 2:13, is unknown apart from the reference here.

Digging In

1. In what sense does Christ hold a double-edged sword? See 2:12. See also 1:16; Ephesians 6:17; and Hebrews 4:12. *The double-edged sword symbolizes the Word of God. It penetrates the heart, judging its thoughts and intentions. God's Word defends the believer from the attacks of Satan.* Is the double-edged sword Law that condemns or Gospel that saves? *The Word of God contains both Law and Gospel. Thus the Law that condemns and the Gospel that saves are two edges of the same sword.*

2. In view of the information presented above, why does the phrase "where Satan's throne is" aptly describe Pergamum? See 2:13. *Idolatry is one of the most prominent characteristics of Pergamum.*

3. What price have the Pergamum Christians paid because they have remained true to Christ? See 2:13b. *An early and faithful witness to Christ, Antipas, was martyred in Pergamum. Tradition says he was slowly roasted to death in a bronze kettle. Thus Pergamum was a city of dangers for Christians.* The word *witness* in Greek literally means "martyr." So many faithful witnesses for Jesus died in the early days of Christianity that to be a witness became synonymous with being one who died for Jesus.

4. The Christians of Pergamum defended the faith at great personal cost, yet they were not without fault. What does John have against them? See 2:14–15. *Some at Pergamum held false beliefs similar to those of Balaam. This led to eating food sacrificed to idols and committing acts of sexual immorality. Others followed the practices of the Nicolaitans, perhaps evidenced by the same behaviors.* For the account of Balaam and Balak, see Numbers 22:1–25; 31:1–16. Scripture gives no further information on the origins or practices of the Nicolaitans. What does the letter to the Christians of Pergamum imply that the church should do about those who teach falsely? *False teaching and practices should not be tolerated by the church.*

5. How will repentance be evidenced? See 2:16. *The members of the congregation will no longer teach or tolerate false doctrine or immoral behavior.* Who

gives the church the right to judge doctrine and behavior? See Matthew 16:13–19; John 20:19–23; 1 Corinthians 5:1–5; 2 Corinthians 2:5–11; Galatians 1:6–9; and 2 John 7–11. *Christ Himself gives the church the authority and responsibility to retain the sins of the unrepentant and forgive the sins of those who repent. He does this through His apostles and pastors.*

6. Meat sacrificed to idols was perhaps all that was available in some Gentile communities. Paul says eating it is alright in most cases. When is it harmful? See 1 Corinthians 8:4–13. *Because there is no God but one, eating meat sacrificed to idols is permissible as long as doing so does not harm a weaker Christian's faith.* What must have been happening at Pergamum to bring about the warning in 2:14? *Christians must have indiscreetly been eating meat sacrificed to idols, causing weaker brethren to slip back into false religion and the immoral practices associated with it.*

7. What does Christ threaten if the Christians at Pergamum do not repent? How will Christ fulfill His threat? See 2:16. *He will come and fight against them with the sword of His mouth.*

8. Those who overcome, that is, those who repent and believe in Christ Jesus, are given two promises. What are they? See 2:17. *Jesus calls Himself the "bread of God . . . who comes down from heaven" (John 6:33). This may mean that the repentant person partakes of Jesus, the true manna from heaven, and enjoys eternal life with Him. A foretaste of this is partaking of Christ in Holy Communion. The "white stone" (2:17) may be a vote of acquittal. A black stone would indicate guilt. One is acquitted by faith in Christ and being baptized into the name of the triune God, the "new name" written on the white stone.*

9. How can one know that he or she is receiving the "white stone"? See John 20:31 and Acts 2:38–39. *Through the means of grace, that is the Word believed and the Sacraments received, one knows he or she is saved.*

THINK ABOUT IT

1. What is the purpose of excommunication? Is it done to publicly retain the sins of unrepentant persons and bar them from Holy Communion, or is it intended to restore individuals to fellowship through repentance and forgiveness?

2. Why is church discipline so seldom practiced these days?

3. What in our culture might be similar to the practices of Balaam and the Nicolaitans?

4. Christians are free to do those things the Word of God neither forbids nor mentions. When should a Christian voluntarily limit this freedom? When should Christians refuse to limit this freedom?

5. How does bearing the name of the triune God in Baptism affect one's daily life?

PRAYER

Gracious Savior, You have delivered me from all my sins through faith in Your sure word of forgiveness. Help me be watchful against all things harmful to me and my brothers and sisters. Give me boldness to turn from sin and live my repentance daily. Thank You that in Baptism the triune God has named me as His own. In Jesus' name I pray. Amen.

LETTER TO THE FOURTH ANGEL

WORDS OF LIFE FOR THYATIRA AND ME

REVELATION 2:18–29

THEME VERSE

"Nevertheless, I have this against you: You tolerate that woman Jezebel, who calls herself a prophetess." Revelation 2:20a

OPENING UP

1. If you were given an all-expenses paid trip to Las Vegas, would you go? Why or why not?

2. Would you join an organization that required you to keep secrets? Why or why not?

3. Describe the strangest religious event you have ever observed.

SETTING THE STAGE

- the city of Thyatira
- Lydia
- religion in Thyatira

DIGGING IN

1. Earlier in the Book of Revelation, Jesus Christ is called the "son of man" (1:13). What is He called in this letter? See 2:18. This is the only time this title is given to Jesus in the Book of Revelation. John may have Daniel's vision of the "son of man" in mind as he describes the Son of God. See Daniel 7:13–14 and Daniel 10:5–6. How is Jesus described here? Contrast these descriptions of Christ in glory with the descriptions of Christ among men that are found in the Gospels.

2. For what does Jesus commend the Thyatiran Christians? See 2:19.

3. Despite their virtues, there is one who misleads the congregation at Thyatira. Who is she? See 2:20. This is not the woman's real name but an epithet, a derogatory label she has earned because of her evil influence. In what ways has this woman misled the congregation?

4. How has Jezebel responded to the time given her to repent? See 2:21.

5. What judgment is in store for Jezebel and "those who commit adultery with her"? See 2:22–23a. Is the adultery she and her followers commit physical, spiritual, or both? See 1 Corinthians 6:15ff. and Ephesians 5:22ff. How are the sins of Jezebel and her followers like those of the Nicolaitans and Balaam and Balak? See 2:6 and 2:14–15.

6. Despite the grave warning of intense suffering, how do you know the grace of God is still available to the followers of Jezebel? See 2:22.

7. When Jezebel and her followers are punished, what will the churches know? See 2:23b. Why does this not teach works righteousness?

8. Verse 24 speaks of "Satan's so-called deep secrets." This may be a reference to an early form of Gnosticism. Gnostics progressively revealed their secret knowledge only to the initiated. How is this different from the Gospel? See Matthew 28:19–20.

9. What are Christians to "hold on to"? See 2:25.

10. The Greek phrase translated as "does My will" in 2:26 literally may be translated as "keeps My works." The works of Christ contrast with those of Jezebel, her followers, and Satan. What promise is given to those who do Christ's will and "overcome"? See 2:26–27. See also 2 Timothy 2:11–13.

11. The quote from Psalm 2:9 in verse 27 sounds harsh. How can this be reconciled to John's teaching that "God is love" in 1 John 4:8?

12. Who or what is the "morning star" promised in 2:28–29?

THINK ABOUT IT

1. What specific Gospel is there in this passage? Explain.

2. Lutherans would say the marks of the church are right preaching of the Word of God and proper administration of the Sacraments. Reformed churches add discipline to these marks. Who is right? Why?

3. Historically Lutherans have opposed membership in lodges. How does Revelation 2:24 relate to this position, if at all? Consider Matthew 28:19–20.

4. How can a Christian maintain a moral lifestyle?

PRAYER

Dear Jesus, daily I struggle with temptation to compromise my faith and the holy life my Baptism calls me to live. Sometimes I have failed. Forgive me. Strengthen me through Word and Sacrament that I might overcome temptation, faithfully serve You, and bear witness to Your saving grace. In Your name I pray. Amen.

LETTER TO THE FOURTH ANGEL

WORDS OF LIFE FOR THYATIRA AND ME

Revelation 2:18–29

(Leader)

THEME VERSE

"Nevertheless, I have this against you: You tolerate that woman Jezebel, who calls herself a prophetess." Revelation 2:20a

OPENING UP

1. If you were given an all-expenses paid trip to Las Vegas, would you go? Why or why not?

2. Would you join an organization that required you to keep secrets? Why or why not?

3. Describe the strangest religious event you have ever observed.

SETTING THE STAGE

- Thyatira is the smallest and least important town in the seven-church circuit, yet it receives the longest letter.

- Founded by the Macedonians, Thyatira was located about 30 miles southeast of Pergamum on the Lycus River. The modern name is Ak-Hissar.

- Thyatira was important not for its arts and culture but as a commercial center. Inscriptions mention wool; linen- and leatherworkers; tanners, dyers, and garment makers; potters; bakers; slave traders; and bronze-smiths.

- Lydia, one of Paul's converts in Philippi, was a dealer in purple cloth who came from Thyatira (Acts 16:13–15).

- By the third century, Thyatira was a stronghold of Montanism, a heretical sect known for its strict asceticism and manifestations of the Holy Spirit through prophets and prophetesses. Perhaps this was in reaction to the religious and moral laxity mentioned in the letter recorded by John in Revelation.

DIGGING IN

1. Earlier in the Book of Revelation Jesus Christ is called the "son of man" (1:13). What is He called here? See 2:18. *"Son of God."* This is the only time this title is given to Jesus in the Book of Revelation. John may have Daniel's vision of the "son of man" in mind as he describes the Son of God. See Daniel 7:13–14 and Daniel 10:5–6. How is Jesus described here? *He comes with the clouds; is led into the presence of the Ancient of Days; is given authority, glory, and sovereign power; all peoples worship Him; and His dominion is everlasting. His body is like chrysolite, His face like lightning, His eyes like flaming torches, His arms and legs like burnished bronze, His voice like a multitude.* Contrast these descriptions of Christ in glory with the descriptions of Christ among men that are found in the Gospels. *Answers will vary.*

2. For what does Jesus commend the Thyatiran Christians? See 2:19. *They are commended for their deeds, love and faith, service and perseverance, and doing more than they did at first.*

3. Despite their virtues, there is one who misleads the congregation at Thyatira. Who is she? See 2:20. *Jezebel.* This is not the woman's real name but an epithet, a derogatory label she has earned because of her evil influence. In what ways has this woman misled the congregation? *See 1 Kings 16:29–34; 18:13; and 2 Kings 9:30–37 for information on the Old Testament Jezebel. She calls herself a prophetess. She misleads the people into sexual immorality and eating food sacrificed to idols.*

4. How has Jezebel responded to the time given her to repent? See 2:21. *She is unwilling.*

5. What judgment is in store for Jezebel and "those who commit adultery with her"? See 2:22–23a. *She will be cast on a bed of suffering. Those who*

commit adultery with her will suffer intensely. Her children, that is, her followers, will be struck dead. Is the adultery she and her followers commit physical, spiritual, or both? See 1 Corinthians 6:15ff. and Ephesians 5:22ff. *Both. Pagan rites incorporated sexual acts. Christians are united to Christ the Bridegroom. Thus to be a Christian and to participate in pagan worship is to commit spiritual adultery.* How are the sins of Jezebel and her followers like those of the Nicolaitans and Balaam and Balak? See 2:6 and 2:14–15. *Participating in pagan worship and sexual immorality are associated with all of these. See Numbers 22–25 for background on Balaam and Balak and immoral pagan worship.*

6. Despite the grave warning of intense suffering, how do you know the grace of God is still available to the followers of Jezebel? See 2:22. *They will suffer intensely "unless they repent." This indicates grace and forgiveness is available to those who do repent.*

7. When Jezebel and her followers are punished, what will the churches know? See 2:23b. *They will know that Christ searches hearts and minds and that He will repay according to one's deeds.* Why does this not teach works righteousness? *Those who will not repent and who reject Christ's gifts of forgiveness and righteousness are judged by their works. Those who do repent and receive Christ's gift of forgiveness and righteousness by faith are judged according to God's grace.*

8. Verse 24 speaks of "Satan's so-called deep secrets." This may be a reference to an early form of Gnosticism. Gnostics progressively revealed their secret knowledge only to the initiated. How is this different from the Gospel? See Matthew 28:19–20. *All nations are to be baptized and taught everything Jesus has commanded. Christians have no secret doctrines or rites. For a summary of gnostic teaching, see the Concordia Self-Study Bible, p. 1925.*

9. What are Christians to "hold on to"? See 2:25. *All those baptized into the name of the triune God are to hold on to the good news of forgiveness of sins and eternal life that is ours through faith in Jesus who died, rose, and is coming again.*

10. The Greek phrase translated as "does My will" in 2:26 literally may be translated as "keeps My works." The works of Christ contrast with those of Jezebel, her followers, and Satan. What promise is given to those who do Christ's will and "overcome"? See 2:26–27. See also 2 Timothy 2:11–13. *Those who do Christ's will, who overcome, and who endure will reign with Christ in glory. That is, they will share in His victory forever in heaven.*

11. The quote from Psalm 2:9 in verse 27 sounds harsh. How can this be reconciled to John's teaching that "God is love" in 1 John 4:8? *Psalm 2:9 and 1 John 4:8 reveal different attributes of God. According to Luther: "God threatens to punish all who break these commandments. . . . But he promises grace and every blessing to those all who keep these commandments" (Luther's Small Catechism). Although everyone breaks God's Law, Christ has died for sinners. There is no need for anyone to suffer punishment, only believe.*

12. Who or what is the "morning star" promised in 2:28–29? *This is Christ, and those who hear will spend eternity with Him.*

Think about It

1. What specific Gospel is there in this passage? Explain.

2. Lutherans would say the marks of the church are right preaching of the Word of God and proper administration of the Sacraments. Reformed churches add discipline to these marks. Who is right? Why?

3. Historically Lutherans have opposed membership in lodges. How does Revelation 2:24 relate to this position, if at all? Consider Matthew 28:19–20.

4. How can a Christian maintain a moral lifestyle?

Prayer

Dear Jesus, daily I struggle with temptation to compromise my faith and the holy life my Baptism calls me to. Sometimes I have failed. Forgive me. Strengthen me through Word and Sacrament that I might overcome temptation, faithfully serve You, and bear witness to Your saving grace. In Your name I pray. Amen.

LETTER TO THE FIFTH ANGEL

WORDS OF LIFE FOR SARDIS AND ME

Revelation 3:1–6

THEME VERSE

"Wake up! Strengthen what remains and is about to die, for I have not found your deeds complete in the sight of My God." Revelation 3:2

OPENING UP

1. Describe a time you arrived at an event only to be turned away because you did not have a reservation. How did you feel? How was the problem solved?

2. What is your favorite method of stain removal? What have you been told works but really doesn't?

3. If your home has ever been broken into, describe the experience. What did it teach you?

SETTING THE STAGE

- the city of Sardis
- the economy of Sardis
- the geography of Sardis
- earthquakes
- religion in Sardis

DIGGING IN

1. Compare the letter to the church at Sardis with the letters to the churches of Smyrna and Pergamum. What problems and errors experi-

enced by those churches are absent in Sardis? How might the location of Sardis figure in to the absence of these problems?

2. Other places in Scripture speak of the Spirit of God as singular. See John 14:16. In what sense is He "seven"? See 3:1. See also Isaiah 11:2.

3. What are the seven "stars"? See 3:1.

4. Although Christ knows the deeds of the congregation, and though the Christians of Sardis have a reputation for being alive, what is really true? See 3:1. Compare Jesus' assessment of the church at Sardis with His opinion of the Pharisees. See Matthew 23:27–28.

5. What admonition and warning does Jesus give the church at Sardis? See 3:2.

6. How can the deeds of the Sardis Christians be made complete? What steps do they need to take? See 3:2–3a. What has the congregation received and heard that will enable its members to wake up, strengthen what remains, obey, and repent? See 1 Corinthians 11:23; Romans 10:17; James 1:18; and Titus 3:3–7.

7. What are the consequences of not heeding the admonition to "wake up"? How is this warning similar to and different than the warning found in the parables in Luke 12:35–48?

8. What portion of the congregation at Sardis is not among those Christ warns? See 3:4. How are they described? What must be true of them that is not true of the others? See 3:4. See also 3:3.

9. What are Christ's assurances to this remnant? See 3:4–5.

10. Why are "white" garments appropriate for the faithful? See 1 Corinthians 6:11.

11. A book in which the names of God's people are recorded is mentioned frequently in Scripture. See Exodus 32:32–33; Psalm 69:28; Revelation 13:8; 20:15; 20:15; and 22:19. Is the imagery of the Book of Life Law or Gospel, threat or good news?

12. How can one know Christ will acknowledge him or her before His Father and His angels? See 3:5b. See also Luke 12:8–9.

13. In summary, how would one demonstrate that he or she has heard what the Spirit says to the churches? See 3:6.

THINK ABOUT IT

1. How are we like the church at Sardis? How are we different from the church at Sardis?

2. What words of comfort and encouragement are in this passage?

3. On reflection, all Christians know they have "soiled their clothes." How can one be sure he or she will be "dressed in white" and acknowledged by Christ before the Father?

4. On what basis will Jesus confess your name before God in heaven?

PRAYER

Savior, Jesus, when I take a good look at myself, I find I am often short on deeds and soiled by sin. I want You to find my deeds complete, my clothes white, and my name in Your book. To that end, open my heart to Your Word, forgive all my sins, work within me true repentance, grant me a living faith that looks only to You for all my righteousness, and help my life overflow with good works that please You. Then Lord, by Your grace, may I know that You acknowledge me before Your Father. In Your name I pray. Amen.

LETTER TO THE FIFTH ANGEL

WORDS OF LIFE FOR SARDIS AND ME

Revelation 3:1–6

(Leader)

THEME VERSE

"Wake up! Strengthen what remains and is about to die, for I have not found your deeds complete in the sight of My God." Revelation 3:2

OPENING UP

1. Describe a time you arrived at an event only to be turned away because you did not have a reservation. How did you feel? How was the problem solved?

2. What's your favorite method of stain removal? What have you been told works but really doesn't?

3. If your home has ever been broken into, describe the experience. What did it teach you?

SETTING THE STAGE

- Sardis was located 30 miles southeast of Thyatira in the circuit of seven churches. Dating from the beginning of the Iron Age, Sardis was ideally suited for commerce because it was situated on an east-west road. The capital of wealthy Lydia, Sardis manufactured textiles, jewelry, and perhaps the world's first coins during the reign of Croesus.

- Although built on a steep hill and fortified with what were thought to be impregnable defenses, Cyrus the Great conquered the city in the sixth century before Christ and Antiochus the Great repeated the feat in the third century before Christ. Both times the attackers scaled the walls at night when the city's defenders lacked vigilance.

- An earthquake destroyed Sardis in A.D. 17, profoundly affecting the overconfident citizens. Sardis was rebuilt with generous aid from the Emperor Tiberius.

- Mystery cults flourished in Sardis, especially worship of Cybele, goddess of the earth and ruler of a race of gods called Titans.

Digging In

1. Compare the letter to the church at Sardis with the letters to the churches of Smyrna and Pergamum. What problems and errors experienced by those churches are absent in Sardis? *There is no mention of persecution, sexual immorality, or idolatry.* How might the location of Sardis figure in to the absence of these problems? *It was relatively remote and difficult to reach.*

2. Other places in Scripture speak of the Spirit of God as singular. See John 14:16. In what sense is He "seven"? See 3:1. See also Isaiah 11:2. *Seven is the number of completion and perfection. The Holy Spirit is thus perfect. Isaiah speaks of (1) the Spirit of the LORD, (2) of wisdom, (3) of understanding, (4) of counsel, (5) of power, (6) of knowledge, and (7) of fear.*

3. What are the seven "stars"? See 3:1. *The seven stars are the seven angels of the seven churches. Angels are messengers, either spiritual beings or pastors.*

4. Although Christ knows the deeds of the congregation, and though the Christians of Sardis have a reputation for being alive, what is really true? See 3:1. *They are dead.* Compare Jesus' assessment of the church at Sardis with His opinion of the Pharisees. See Matthew 23:27–28. *The Pharisees appear beautiful on the outside but are full of dead men's bones on the inside. They only appear righteous but are in fact wicked. The church at Sardis resembles the Pharisees.*

5. What admonition and warning does Jesus give the church at Sardis? See 3:2. *"Wake up! Strengthen what remains and is about to die."*

6. How can the deeds of the Sardis Christians be made complete? What steps do they need to take? See 3:2–3a. *They need to (1) wake up; (2) strengthen what remains; (3) remember what they have received and heard; (4)*

obey; and (5) repent. What has the congregation received and heard that will enable its members to wake up, strengthen what remains, obey, and repent? See 1 Corinthians 11:23; Romans 10:17; James 1:18; and Titus 3:3–7. *The Word of God and the sacraments of Baptism and the Lord's Supper give us all we need for salvation and to live a God-pleasing life. The Sardis Christians, and all of us, need to return to these means of grace.*

7. What are the consequences of not heeding the admonition to "wake up"? *Christ will come like a thief. Chastening is implied.* How is this warning similar to and different than the warning found in the parables in Luke 12:35–48? *The warning to Sardis is similar to the warning in the parables because the master goes away, entrusting his possessions to his servants, expecting them to be watchful for his return and faithful to keep his charge to them. The warning is different because Christ comes to Sardis conditionally, that is, if they do not repent. The parables deal with the return of Christ at the end of the age.*

8. What portion of the congregation at Sardis is not among those Christ warns? See 3:4. *A few.* How are they described? *They have "not soiled their clothes."* What must be true of them that is not true of the others? See 3:4. See also 3:3. *Those who by God's grace have not soiled their clothes are worthy. They are awake, they remember what they have received and heard in Word and Sacrament, they obey, and they live in repentance.*

9. What are Christ's assurances to this remnant? See 3:4–5. *(1) They will walk with Christ, dressed in white. (2) They are worthy. (3) Their names will never be blotted from the Book of Life. (4) Christ will acknowledge their names before His Father.*

10. Why are "white" garments appropriate for the faithful? See 1 Corinthians 6:11. *In Holy Baptism, sinners are washed and sanctified, that is, made holy. They are clothed with Christ and His righteousness. White symbolizes this purity. Note that in the ancient church, white robes were placed on the newly baptized.*

11. A book in which the names of God's people are recorded is mentioned frequently in Scripture. See Exodus 32:32–33; Psalm 69:28; Revelation 13:8; 20:15; 20:15; and 22:19. Is the imagery of the Book of Life Law or Gospel, threat or good news? *The implication is that the unrepentant are blotted out of the Book of Life but the repentant, who are saved by Christ as evidenced by their deeds, are listed forever in the Book of Life. The former is Law, the latter Gospel.*

12. How can one know Christ will acknowledge him or her before His Father and His angels? See 3:5b. See also Luke 12:8–9. *Christ acknowledges those who acknowledge Him but disowns those who disown Him.*

13. In summary, how would one demonstrate that he or she has heard what the Spirit says to the churches? See 3:6. *One who hears is repentant, watchful, obedient, characterized by good deeds, and unsoiled, all of which is worked in the believer through the means of grace, Word and Sacrament.*

THINK ABOUT IT

1. How are we like the church at Sardis? How are we different from the church at Sardis?

2. What words of comfort and encouragement are in this passage?

3. On reflection, all Christians know they have "soiled their clothes." How can one be sure he or she will be "dressed in white" and acknowledged by Christ before the Father?

4. On what basis will Jesus confess your name before God in heaven?

PRAYER

Savior, Jesus, when I take a good look at myself, I find I am often short on deeds and soiled by sin. I want You to find my deeds complete, my clothes white, and my name in Your book. To that end, open my heart to Your Word, forgive all my sins, work within me true repentance, grant me a living faith that looks only to You for all my righteousness, and help my life overflow with good works that please You. Then Lord, by Your grace, may I know that You acknowledge me before Your Father. In Your name I pray. Amen.

LETTER TO THE SIXTH ANGEL

WORDS OF LIFE
FOR PHILADELPHIA AND ME

Revelation 3:7–13

THEME VERSE

"I am coming soon. Hold on to what you have, so that no one will take your crown." Revelation 3:11

OPENING UP

1. In what part of the country have you found the most friendly and loving people?

2. When have you sensed God keeping you through a time of trial?

3. Describe a great building you have seen. What impressed you the most? Why?

SETTING THE STAGE

- the city of Philadelphia
- the geography of Philadelphia
- the history of Philadelphia
- the culture of Philadelphia

DIGGING IN

1. Scan the letter. How are the Christians at Philadelphia like the church at Smyrna? See 2:8–11.

2. How would the description of Christ as "holy and true" reassure the struggling Christians in Philadelphia? See 3:1.

3. Why would David's "key" be associated with Christ in 3:7?

4. What does the key of David held by Jesus open and shut? See 3:7. See also Matthew 16:19 and John 20:23. How would this reassure struggling Christians?

5. Verse 8 implies that someone is trying to shut the door to God's forgiveness and eternal life. Who might that be? See 3:9.

6. What has Christ observed about the Philadelphian Christians? See 3:8. The Greek word *dynamis* may be translated as "strength" or "power." What are some possible ways the congregation is lacking in strength or power? Note that though the congregation may have little power, Christ says it has not "denied My name."

7. Jews claimed a special relationship with God by virtue of descent from Abraham. What is Christ's assessment of unbelieving Jews at Philadelphia? See 3:9. According to Jesus, who is the father of such Jews? See John 8:44. Who is a true child of Abraham? See Romans 4:16 and Galatians 3:7.

8. What will unbelieving Jews who trouble the Christians someday acknowledge? See 3:9. Will this be voluntary or forced?

9. An "hour of trial" is coming on the whole world. See 3:10. There are three possible interpretations: (1) Roman persecution of Christians in the second and third centuries; (2) repeated persecutions throughout history; (3) or a time of great tribulation prior to the second coming of Christ. Whenever it might be, what promise does Christ make to believers in "the hour of trial"?

10. What incentives do suffering Christians have to remain faithful? See 3:11–12. As in 2:10, the "crown" in this verse is the victor's wreath, not the diadem worn by royalty. When are the names signifying ownership by God written on the Christian? See Matthew 28:19.

11. How do you know that the words in this letter are not directed only to the congregation at Philadelphia but to the seven churches and every other church? See 3:13.

THINK ABOUT IT

1. When have you been so weakened by trials that you felt like giving up? What kept you going?

2. Lutherans speak of the "Office of the Keys" as that power Christ gives to His church to forgive or retain sins, a power exercised through pastors. How important are "the keys" to you? What is the implication for church membership and worship attendance?

3. What difference does the size of a congregation make to you? What blessings are available to you regardless of size?

4. How should you, a Christian, relate to Jews who as yet do not accept Jesus as the Messiah?

5. A bumper sticker says, "In case of the rapture, the driver of this car will disappear." Respond.

PRAYER

Jesus, Your promises to me are sure. They hold all the encouragement I need to remain faithful. Help me trust them. May I always remember that You have claimed me as Your own in Baptism. In Your name I pray. Amen.

LETTER TO THE SIXTH ANGEL

WORDS OF LIFE
FOR PHILADELPHIA AND ME

Revelation 3:7–13

(Leader)

THEME VERSE

"I am coming soon. Hold on to what you have, so that no one will take your crown." Revelation 3:11

OPENING UP

1. In what part of the country have you found the most friendly and loving people?

2. When have you sensed God keeping you through a time of trial?

3. Describe a great building you have seen. What impressed you the most? Why?

SETTING THE STAGE

- The city of Philadelphia, meaning "brotherly love," was located 30 miles southeast of Sardis at the junction of three important roads. It was a gateway to the east. The name commemorates the loyalty of Attalus II of Pergamum to his brother Eumenes II. Ala-Sheher, the modern name, means "city of God."

- Attalus intended that the city would promote the Hellenistic way of life. It was a center for the cult of Dionysus, but temples to other gods also existed. A staple of the economy was grape growing.

- The sixth church in the circuit of seven, Philadelphia had seen its share of catastrophic earthquakes. Pillars in the pagan temples had no doubt fallen, something that will not happen to faithful Christians who become pillars in the temple of God. See 3:12.

- Philadelphia's Greco-Roman culture endured until A.D. 1390 when the city fell to Bajazet I. Ruins of many ancient churches can be seen there today.

DIGGING IN

1. Scan the letter. How are the Christians at Philadelphia like the church at Smyrna? See 2:8–11. *There is no explicit criticism in this letter. The Christians of Philadelphia face the same enemy, the "synagogue of Satan."*

2. How would the description of Christ as "holy and true" reassure the struggling Christians in Philadelphia? See 3:7. *"Holy" equates Christ with God, who is morally perfect. "True" affirms Christ's total trustworthiness. As the divine Savior, Jesus can be trusted to do what is right and good on behalf of the struggling Christians.*

3. Why would David's "key" be associated with Christ in 3:7? *David is Israel's ideal king and a type of Christ. Jesus, the descendant of David, holds all the kingly power of David, which is symbolized by the key.*

4. What does the key of David held by Jesus open and shut? See 3:7. See also Matthew 16:19 and John 20:23. *The key of David is the authority and power to open or shut heaven, to forgive or to retain sins.* How would this reassure struggling Christians? *Despite the trials of life and attacks on one's faith, the believer is assured that Jesus has opened heaven's door. It will not be shut but will remain open and welcome the believer home.*

5. Revelation 3:8 implies that someone is trying to shut the door to God's forgiveness and eternal life. Who might that be? See 3:9 *These are Jews who bar Christians from the synagogue and deny that they are loved by God.*

6. What has Christ observed about the Philadelphian Christians? See 3:8. *He has observed their deeds, that they have little strength or power, and that they have not denied His name.* The Greek word *dynamis* may be translated as "strength" or "power." What are some possible ways the congregation is lacking in strength or power? *It may be a small congregation with little influence. It may be weakened by constant persecution and feel like giving up.* Note

that though the congregation may have little power, Christ says it has not "denied My name."

7. Jews claimed a special relationship with God by virtue of descent from Abraham. What is Christ's assessment of unbelieving Jews at Philadelphia? See 3:9. *They are a "synagogue of Satan." They claim to be Jews but are not. They are liars.* According to Jesus, who is the father of such Jews? See John 8:44. *"You belong to your father, the devil."* Who is a true child of Abraham? See Romans 4:16 and Galatians 3:7. *All who are righteous by faith in Jesus Christ are children of Abraham, both Jew and Gentile.*

8. What will unbelieving Jews who trouble the Christians someday acknowledge? See 3:9. *They will fall at the feet of the Christians and acknowledge that Christ loves them.* Will this be voluntary or forced? *It is probably a forced act, perhaps on the day of Christ's return.*

9. An "hour of trial" is coming on the whole world, See 3:10. There are three possible interpretations: (1) Roman persecution of Christians in the second and third centuries; (2) repeated persecutions throughout history; (3) or a time of great tribulation prior to the second coming of Christ. Whenever it might be, what promise does Christ make to believers in "the hour of trial"? *"I will also keep you from the hour of trial that is going to come upon the whole world." "I will also keep you from the hour of trial" is better translated "I will also keep you through the hour of trial." The former translation is preferred by those who teach a pre-tribulation rapture. This is the idea that Christians will be taken to heaven before the tribulation. Lutherans reject this, believing that Christians will go through tribulation, but be protected from every evil that would separate us from Christ. See John 15:20 and Romans 8:35–39.*

10. What incentives do suffering Christians have to remain faithful? See 3:11–12. *(1) Jesus is coming soon. (2) Those who hold on to what they have in Christ will keep their crown. (3) Believers will be pillars in the temple of God, a temple God will never again leave. (4) They will have written on them the names of God, the city of God, which is the new Jerusalem, and Christ's new name.* As in 2:10, the "crown" in this verse is the victor's wreath, not the diadem worn by royalty. When are the names signifying ownership by God written on the Christian? See Matthew 28:19. *The names of God are placed on Christians at Baptism, assuring them that they are His.*

11. How do you know that the words in this letter are not directed only to the congregation at Philadelphia but to the seven churches and every other church? See 3:13. *"Churches" is plural.*

THINK ABOUT IT

1. When have you been so weakened by trials that you felt like giving up? What kept you going?

2. Lutherans speak of the "Office of the Keys" as that power Christ gives to His church to forgive or retain sins, a power exercised through pastors. How important are "the keys" to you? What is the implication for church membership and worship attendance?

3. What difference does the size of a congregation make to you? What blessings are available to you regardless of size?

4. How should you, a Christian, relate to Jews who as yet do not accept Jesus as the Messiah?

5. A bumper sticker says, "In case of the rapture, the driver of this car will disappear." Respond.

PRAYER

Jesus, Your promises to me are sure. They hold all the encouragement I need to remain faithful. Help me trust them. May I always remember that You have claimed me as Your own in Baptism. In Your name I pray. Amen.

LETTER TO THE SEVENTH ANGEL

WORDS OF LIFE FOR LAODICEA AND ME

Revelation 3:14–22

THEME VERSE

"You are neither cold nor hot. I wish you were either one or the other!"
Revelation 3:15

OPENING UP

1. Would you drink a can of room-temperature soda? Explain.

2. Grandma's birthday is coming. She says, "Don't get me anything. I have all I need." What do you do?

3. When you hear a knock at the door, are you curious, annoyed, frightened, or delighted? How do you decide whether to open the door?

SETTING THE STAGE

- the city of Laodicea

- the history of Laodicea

- Christianity in Laodicea

DIGGING IN

1. List three titles Christ gives to Himself in 3:14. "Amen" is a Hebrew word that affirms the truth of a statement. By identifying Himself as "the Amen," what is Jesus affirming about Himself? The Greek word for "martyr" is translated here as "witness." In bearing witness to God's truth, what happened to Jesus? The Greek word *arche* means "ruler" and here refers to Christ as the source, beginning, or chief of all creation. Because all this is true of Christ, who is He?

2. What is Christ's admonition to the church at Laodicea? See 3:15. The Greek word *zestos* means "hot." From *zestos*, we get *zest* or *zesty*. Medicinal hot springs were located near Laodicea. What other healing water of even greater value are the Laodiceans overlooking? What apparently is true of their faith and life as Christians? Why would Christ actually prefer them to be cold if not hot?

3. If neither hot nor cold, what are the Laodiceans? See 3:16. What warning does Christ give them? The Greek word translated as "spit" can also be translated as "vomit." What does this imply about the standing the Laodiceans have before God?

4. How do the Laodiceans view themselves? See 3:17. What is their true condition? How does their economic and spiritual status compare with the church at Smyrna? See 2:9.

5. What is Christ's counsel to the congregation? See 3:18, which is rich in allusions to other Scripture passages. Laodicea may be rich, but what do the people of this city need that can never be bought with money? See Isaiah 52:3; 55:1–2; Ephesians 2:8–9; and Titus 3:5–6. Gold refined with fire contrasts with the products that made Laodicea rich. Refined gold endures. What item that the Laodiceans need does gold symbolize? Where can the Laodiceans get the white clothes they need to cover their shameful nakedness? See Galatians 3:26–29. Why is it ironic that the Laodiceans need to buy eye salve so they can see? How are the people blind? Compare with John 10:39–41.

6. Christ has strong words for the people of Laodicea, yet what is His relationship to them? See 3:19. See also Hebrews 12:4–11. What does Christ want from the people of Laodicea?

7. Is the promise in 3:20 made to non-Christians or to lukewarm believers? How does this distinction affect the meaning of the verse? Which means of grace may be suggested as important to maintaining fervent faith? See 3:20b.

8. What great blessing awaits those who overcome the temptations of lukewarm faith? See 3:21. Contrast what Christ overcame with what the Laodiceans must overcome.

9. How can the churches "hear what the Spirit says"?

Think about It

1. How are the temptations the Laodiceans faced like the ones we face today?

2. For whom do you think repentance and faithfulness are harder: those who are well-off and face few trials in life or those who are poor, unemployed, sick, etc.?

3. What words of Gospel comfort can we find in this passage?

4. How are the sacraments referred to in this text?

Prayer

Jesus, forgive me for lukewarm faith that neither fears God's wrath nor cherishes His grace. Move me by Word and Sacrament that I might know both the dangers of my sin and the joy of Your forgiveness. In Your name I pray. Amen.

LETTER TO THE SEVENTH ANGEL

WORDS OF LIFE FOR LAODICEA AND ME

Revelation 3:14–22

(Leader)

THEME VERSE

"You are neither cold nor hot. I wish you were either one or the other!"
Revelation 3:15

OPENING UP

1. Would you drink a can of room-temperature soda? Explain.

2. Grandma's birthday is coming. She says, "Don't get me anything. I have all I need." What do you do?

3. When you hear a knock at the door, are you curious, annoyed, frightened, or delighted? How do you decide whether to open the door?

BACKGROUND

- Laodicea lies in a valley at the junction of the Lycus and Maeander Rivers and at the intersection of three major roads. Five of the seven churches were located on one of these roads. The gateway to Phrygia, Laodicea had grown wealthy from banking, clothing manufacture, and black wool cloth.

- Men Carou, a god of healing, was the patron deity of the city. Laodicea's medical school and eye and ear ointments were famous. There was a thriving emperor cult in the city. Thousands of Jews freely practiced their religion in Laodicea.

- Epaphras may have started the church in Laodicea. See Colossians 1:7. A letter from Paul to the Laodiceans has been lost. See Colossians 4:16.

- The modern name of Laodicea is Eski-hisar.

DIGGING IN

1. List three titles Christ gives to Himself in 3:14. *The Amen, the faithful and true witness, the ruler of God's creation.* "Amen" is a Hebrew word that affirms the truth of a statement. By identifying Himself as "the Amen," what is Jesus affirming about Himself? *His complete trustworthiness.* The Greek word for "martyr" is translated here as "witness." In bearing witness to God's truth, what happened to Jesus? *Jesus was crucified.* The Greek word *arche* means "ruler" and here refers to Christ as the source, beginning, or chief of all creation. Because all this is true of Christ, who is He? *God.*

2. What is Christ's admonition to the church at Laodicea? See 3:15. *They are neither hot nor cold. He would rather they be one or the other.* What is Christ's admonition to the church at Laodicea? See 3:15. The Greek word *zestos* means "hot." From *zestos*, we get *zest* or *zesty.* Medicinal hot springs were located near the city of Laodicea. What other healing water of even greater value are the Laodiceans overlooking? *The healing water of life in Christ, found in the Sacrament of Holy Baptism.* What apparently is true of their faith and life as Christians? *They are blandly indifferent.* Why would Christ actually prefer them to be cold if not hot? *For their benefit, Christ would have them know whether they are hot or cold, saved or lost. There is no middle ground.*

3. If neither hot nor cold, what are the Laodiceans? See 3:16. *Lukewarm.* What warning does Christ give them? *"I will spit you out of My mouth."* The Greek word translated as "spit" can also be translated as "vomit." What does this imply about the standing the Laodiceans have before God? *They may in fact be lost.*

4. How do the Laodiceans view themselves? See 3:17. *They are rich and need nothing.* What is their true condition? *Spiritually, they are wretched, poor, blind, and naked.* How does their economic and spiritual status compare with the church at Smyrna? See 2:9. *Smyrna is poor in material things but rich spiritually. Laodicea is wealthy materially but poor spiritually.*

5. What is Christ's counsel to the congregation? See 3:18, which is rich in

allusions to other Scripture passages. *"Buy from Me gold refined in the fire, so you can become rich; and white clothes to wear, so you can cover your shameful nakedness; and salve to put on your eyes, so you can see."* Laodicea may be rich, but what do the people of this city need that can never be bought with money? See Isaiah 52:3; 55:1–2; Ephesians 2:8–9; and Titus 3:5–6. *What the people of Laodicea need most is redemption, that is, deliverance from the slavery of sin. This cannot be bought with money or good works but comes only as a gift of God's grace through faith in Christ.* Gold refined with fire contrasts with the products that made Laodicea rich. Refined gold endures. What item that the Laodiceans need does gold symbolize? *It symbolizes the price paid by Jesus for the salvation of sinners.* Where can the Laodiceans get the white clothes they need to cover their shameful nakedness? See Galatians 3:26–29. *Through Holy Baptism, believers are clothed with the righteousness of Christ, made children of God and heirs to all the promises of salvation.* Why is it ironic that the Laodiceans need to buy eye salve so they can see? *Laodicea was famous for its eye ointments and its medical school, yet the people are blind.* How are the people blind? Compare with John 10:39–41. *They have not comprehended their own spiritual blindness and need for Christ, who alone can make them see.*

6. Christ has strong words for the people of Laodicea, yet what is His relationship to them? See 3:19. See also Hebrews 12:4–11. *Christ loves them, otherwise He would not rebuke or discipline them. Christ's loving discipline will produce a harvest of righteousness in those who repent.* What does Christ want from the people of Laodicea? *Repentance.*

7. Is the promise in 3:20 made to non-Christians or to lukewarm believers? *Lukewarm believers.* How does this distinction affect the meaning of the verse? *The meaning is not that non-Christians should invite Jesus in but that Christ awaits an invitation to join those who already know Him by faith.* Which means of grace may be suggested as important to maintaining fervent faith? See 3:20b. *Holy Communion.*

8. What great blessing awaits those who overcome the temptations of lukewarm faith? See 3:21. *"To him who overcomes, I will give the right to sit with Me on My throne."* Contrast what Christ overcame with what the Laodiceans must overcome. *Christ overcame the cross and the grave. The Laodiceans must overcome the temptations of riches, self-righteousness, and lukewarm, indifferent faith.*

9. How can the churches "hear what the Spirit says"? *Word and Sacrament are the means of grace through which the churches hear.*

THINK ABOUT IT

1. How are the temptations the Laodiceans faced like the ones we face today?

2. For whom do you think repentance and faithfulness are harder: those who are well-off and face few trials in life or those who are poor, unemployed, sick, etc.?

3. What words of Gospel comfort can we find in this passage?

4. How are the sacraments referred to in this text?

PRAYER

Jesus, forgive me for lukewarm faith that neither fears God's wrath nor cherishes His grace. Move me by Word and Sacrament that I might know both the dangers of my sin and the joy of Your forgiveness. In Your name I pray. Amen.